Edward Gorey

HIS BOOK COVER ART & DESIGN

Essay by **Steven Heller**

PORTLAND, OREGON

Thanks to Edward Bradford, Andreas Brown, Steven Heller, and Consuelo Joerns for their vital contributions to the content and design of this book.

Pomegranate Communications, Inc.
19018 NE Portal Way, Portland OR 97230
800 227 1428 • www.pomegranate.com

Pomegranate Europe Ltd.
Unit 1, Heathcote Business Centre, Hurlbutt Road
Warwick, Warwickshire CV34 6TD, UK
[+44] 0 1926 430111 • sales@pomeurope.co.uk

To learn about new releases and special offers from Pomegranate, please visit www.pomegranate.com and sign up for our e-mail newsletter. For all other queries, see "Contact Us" on our home page.

© 2015 The Edward Gorey Charitable Trust. Published under license from
The Edward Gorey Charitable Trust.
Essay © 2015 Steven Heller
An **Edward Gorey**® licensed product.
All rights reserved.

The contents of this book are protected by copyright, including all images and all text. This copyrighted material may not be reproduced or transmitted in any form or by any means, electronic or mechanical, including but not limited to photocopying, scanning, recording, or by any information storage or retrieval system, without the express permission in writing of the copyright holders.

FRONT COVER: *Lafcadio's Adventures*, Doubleday Anchor, 1953; *Old Possum's Book of Practical Cats*, Harcourt Brace Jovanovich, 1982; *Amerika*, Doubleday Anchor, 1955; *Come Back, Dr. Caligari*, Doubleday Anchor, 1965; and *From Beowulf to Virginia Woolf*, Charter Books, 1963
TITLE PAGE: Edward Gorey's business card, unpublished, c. 1964
BACK COVER: *True Tales from the Annals of Crime and Rascality*, Vintage Books, 1957; *The Sot-Weed Factor*, Doubleday, 1960; *A Hero of Our Time*, Doubleday Anchor, 1956; *The War of the Worlds*, Looking Glass Library, 1960; and *Nineteenth Century German Tales*, Doubleday Anchor, 1959

THIS BOOK'S CAPTIONS USE THE FOLLOWING ABBREVIATIONS: "HC" for hardcover, "PB" for paperback, and "Text illus." to indicate that Gorey also created illustrations within text.

Library of Congress Cataloging-in-Publication Data
Heller, Steven.
 Edward Gorey : his book cover art and design / By Steven Heller.
    pages cm
 Includes index.
 ISBN 978-0-7649-7147-1 (alk. paper)
1. Gorey, Edward, 1925-2000--Criticism and interpretation. 2. Book cover art--United States. I. Title.
NC975.5.G6H45 2015
741.6'4092--dc23
                    2014036745

Pomegranate Item No. A239

Designed by Patrice Morris

Printed in China

24 23 22 21 20 19 18 17 16 15   10 9 8 7 6 5 4 3 2 1

Contents

Edward Gorey's Cover Story
by Steven Heller   5

Index of Book Titles   132

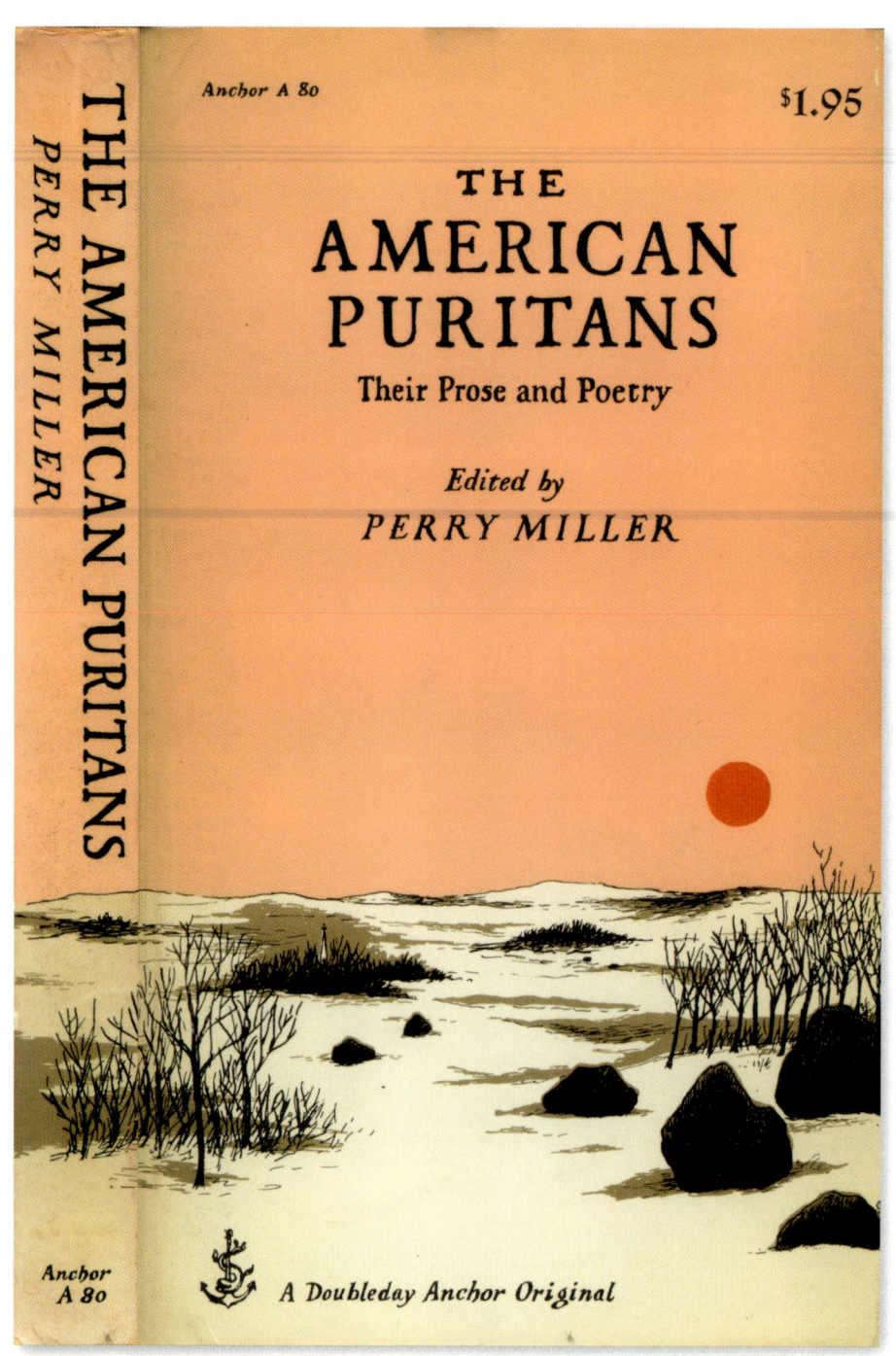

The American Puritans: Their Prose and Poetry edited by Perry Miller
Doubleday Anchor, 1956, PB

Edward Gorey's Cover Story
Steven Heller

Deliciously and subversively cryptic, Edward St. John Gorey's iconic books, plays, postcards, toys, stage sets, and costumes—indeed an entire lifetime of utterly sublime, mockingly apprehensive artistry and authorship—are duly celebrated and critically acclaimed by everyone from cultural pundits to Goth cultists. The rare front-page *New York Times* obituary, on April 17, 2000, is testament to Gorey's eclectic narrative range. "In creating a large body of small work, he made an indelible imprint on noir fiction and on the psyche of his admirers," Mel Gussow reported. Yet understandably, less attention is devoted today to the more than 200 illustrated paperback covers and hardcover jackets that Chicago-born, Harvard-educated Gorey (known to his friends as Ted) created while working as a staff artist in Doubleday Anchor's art department, art director and editor at Random House's Looking Glass Library, art director at Bobbs-Merrill (which Gorey called "Boobs Muddle"), and as a freelance illustrator throughout a large portion of his career.

In two brief sentences, his obituary tossed aside this impressive output: "After graduation he remained in Boston, illustrating book jackets. Then he went to New York and worked in the art department at Doubleday, staying late in the office to create his own books." Still, these pen-and-ink crosshatched and hand-lettered gems from the nascence of his more than fifty-year career arguably challenged prevailing American publishing conventions while they helped define Anchor's and other publishers' visual identities. His covers also unleashed a troupe of melancholy Victorians and Edwardians, woeful infants and tykes, and eerie reptilian and mammalian beasts that haunted his proto–graphic novel "novels," which earned legions of loyal fans over the ensuing decades.

Commercial book cover design is, admittedly, a minor portion of Gorey's award-winning legacy, but not a lesser art. His linear expression and droll comedy are integral ingredients. There are also covers that are stunning for their hidden allusions. The barren landscape, for example, on the cover of *The American Puritans* evokes an otherworldly quietude, but speaks to concealed psychological demons as well. Although these works are perceived as less significant because he was responding to assignments from editors to illustrate other artists' creative offerings, at the very least they serve as historical markers of Gorey's evolving artistic persona. Yet some covers, such as the one for Alain-Fournier's *The Wanderer* (p. 7), have artistic integrity both on *and* beyond the specific volume.

A self-described inveterate reader of prose and poetry (an understatement, since at his death he possessed a twenty-five-thousand-volume personal library), he effortlessly mastered the interpretive challenges endemic to book cover art, while injecting tics and quirks for his own amusement. Gorey's covers and jackets were not done anonymously or as mere throwaways, as many others often were. Nor was this a strategic compromise until he found and embraced his true calling. Today, this body of work exemplifies his unique contribution to a truly exceptional era of graphic design when book covers and jackets became an innovative genre honored by exhibitions and awards.

Nonetheless, paperback covers and hardback dust jackets have a long tradition of being designed by someone other than the interior book designer. This aesthetic-cum-philosophical division of labor derived from the fact that these coverings, designed to sell "units" (as purveyors of books often refer to their stock), were advertising department tools—the products of middle- and lowbrow marketing experts and slaves to the vicissitudes thereof. Orthodox book designers—masters of the typographic arts—rarely deigned to step into the commercial muck lest their pristine typography be compromised by crass requisites of sales and judged accordingly.

But successful cover design requires the expertise of an artist, typographer, poster designer, and logo maker. Many book design specialists were incapable of designing a cover or jacket with the same Gorey aplomb, even if they tried. He routinely asked to create entire books, from jackets and spines to endpapers, title pages, and interiors, in order to achieve aesthetic uniformity. He was usually told no, but persisted and on occasion he "styled" the whole shebang. When it came to his own books, everything was obviously in his hands.

Until sometime in the 1950s, it was tacitly accepted—among both publishers and readers—that dust jackets, like banana peels and gift-wrapping paper, ostensibly existed to be removed and discarded once they served their intended purpose: to attract customers, induce sales, and protect bindings from the ravages of wear and tear. While more or less the same is true today, these dispensable coverings evolved through the late 1940s and 1950s into indispensable appendages. Many have survived, owing to their inescapable allure. In some instances, the cover or jacket image became the book's most identifiable trait, like a logo or product label. This is true with one of Gorey's most popular jackets, *Old Possum's Book of Practical Cats* by T. S. Eliot (1982) (pp. 8–9), which Gorey also entirely illustrated. The book would not be the same without its jacket. (Gorey was, in fact, rigorously screened by Eliot's widow before he was approved as the text and cover artist.)

Fortunately, for scholars interested in covers and jackets, the Library of Congress maintains the practice of archiving almost every published jacket to preserve some kind of historical record. These days, jackets are rarely orphaned as they once were.

Paperbacks were even lower in the book design and packaging pecking order than hardcover jackets. When inexpensive mass-market paperbacks were introduced in the United States in the late 1930s, publishers heralded their ephemerality as commercial boons, while acknowledging they were destined for the junk heap. This practice began to radically change during the late 1940s when some early "quality" or trade paperback publishing companies proffered that their cover designs had a profound impact on their readers' acquisition impulses and intimate relationships with their books.

Anchor Books, founded in 1953, ostensibly started a new wave, followed shortly after by New Directions, Meridian, Noonday, and Vintage, among the most notable. Each published reprint of the classics, as well as serious fiction and nonfiction, was affordably

The Wanderer by Alain-Fournier
Doubleday Anchor, 1953, PB

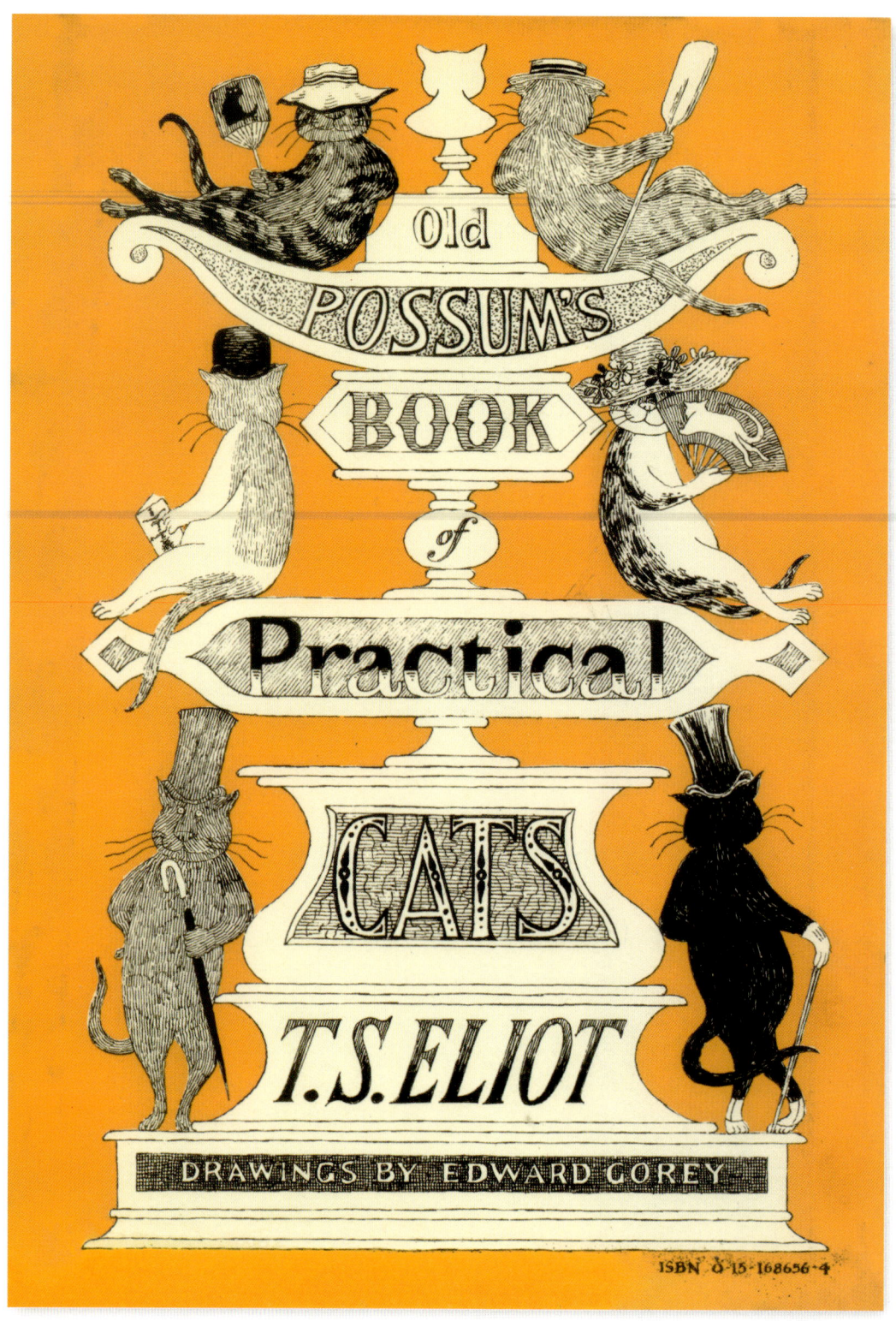

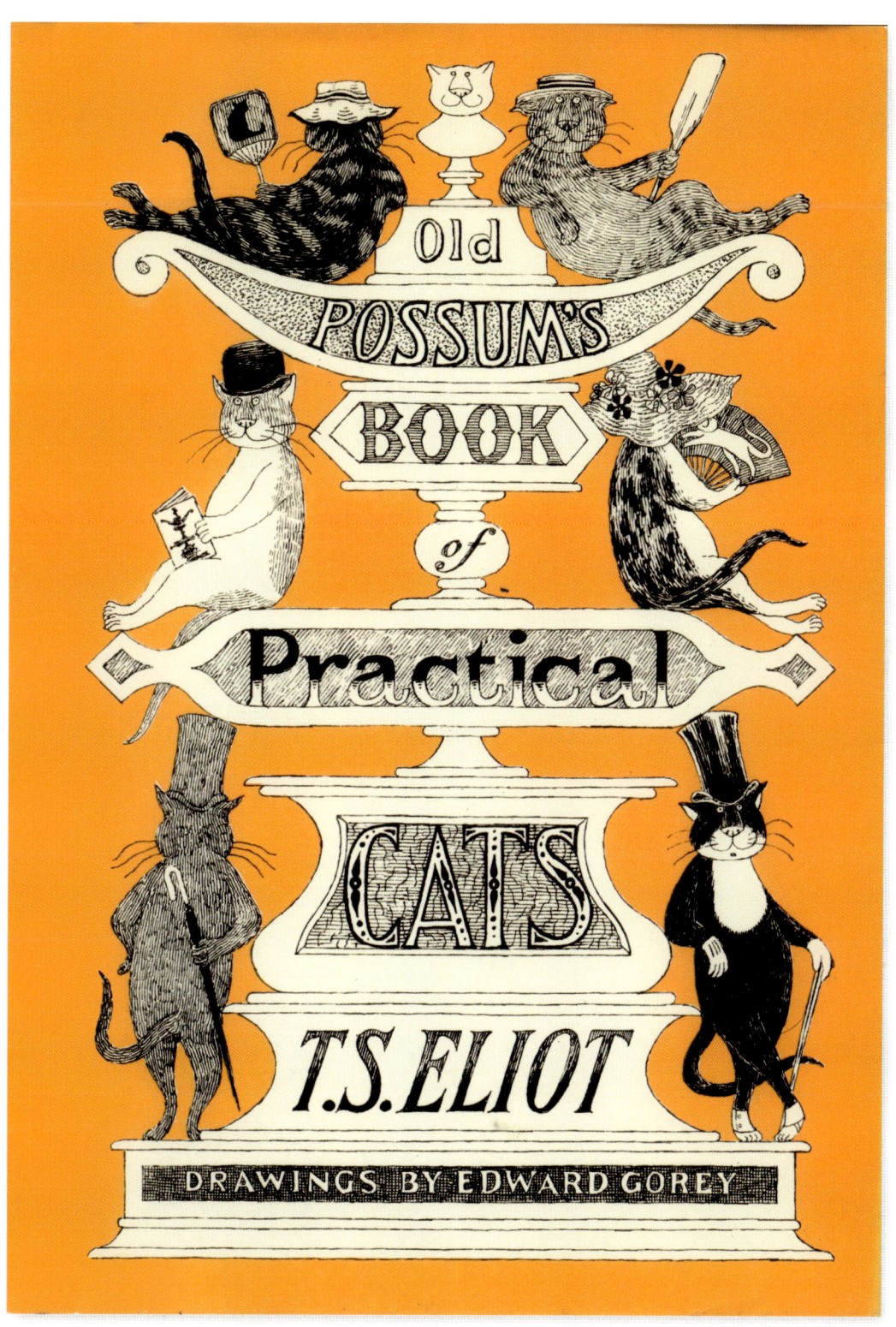

Old Possum's Book of Practical Cats by T. S. Eliot
Harcourt Brace Jovanovich, 1982, HC, text illus.

priced and aimed at a sophisticated audience of college students and other earnest general readers. Printed on quality paper and with sturdier bindings than mass-market books, they employed urbane visual languages characterized by conceptual, surreal, and abstract illustrations, complemented by spare modernist typography. These premium embellishments elevated the status of the books but did not rarify them.

Creative opportunities for designers, typographers, artists, and illustrators increased, not only to create more one-off freelance assignments but to develop distinct house styles. Uniform series altered store display and book-buying conventions, too. Handsomely designed series motivated bookstore managers to exhibit complementary books together, rather than routinely shelve them with their spines facing outward, resulting in the integration of paperbacks and hardbacks on the same table.

Modern less-is-more design proved to be one of the enticing lures for the book-buying public. Mid-century modernist book cover designers, among them Paul Rand, Alvin Lustig, Leo Lionni, George Giusti, Ben Shahn, and others, were appreciated by publishers and their marketing minions. They were given license to experiment with abstract expressionist, Dada, de Stijl, and Bauhaus influences. But the modern manner shared the stage with various other styles that projected "quality" and distinguished themselves from mass-market pulpism. Looking at the avant-garde-inspired paperback covers today—not hamstrung by hard-sell, commercial formulas—they are paradigms of applied modernism and harbingers of future modern publishing tastes.

Gorey would, however, chortle at being associated with what one classical-style book designer called those "Bauhaus boys." Gorey's nineteenth- and early twentieth-century English neo-Gothic credentials were unassailable. As far as draftsmanship goes, he was inspired by early twentieth-century English artist, illustrator, and author Edward Ardizzone, whose own nineteenth-century-inspired, crosshatched, linear and watercolor styles, though somewhat looser than Gorey's, graced the covers and interiors of many early to mid-twentieth-century books and were mainstays in Gorey's personal library. "I had a penchant for the British and was aware of British book jackets because I bought a lot of British books at the time," he said. English contemporaries of Ardizzone, including linear maestros Edward Bawden, Rex Whistler, John Piper, and Paul Nash, whose work captured the hell of trench warfare during World War I, probably gave Gorey more to either reference or parody. He did not directly mimic but rather incorporated certain attributes. There was also a keen interest in the great Sir John Tenniel, whose illustrations for Lewis Carroll's two *Alice* books were expertly wood engraved by the Brothers Dalziel, who Gorey told friends that he greatly admired for injecting life into Tenniel's pencil lines on the printed page. Gorey's work was not pastiche but evoked his passion for the trappings of a particularly romanticized yet cautiously melancholy epoch. Gorey's work was not a priori lugubrious—but rather joyfully dark.

He reserved high admiration for George Herriman, artist and writer of the decidedly modern comic strip *Krazy Kat*, which was amplified when Gorey stumbled upon and retrieved from a Doubleday trash bin Herriman's original drawings illustrating Don Marquis's witty poetic tales of *archy and mehitabel*, a cockroach and alley cat who, through their antics, commented on New York daily life. Gorey saved a few, though wished he'd taken more, which presumably were thrown out. "I could scream now, because nobody knew they were there, and I anguished but finally took three of them," he once recalled. "We were cleaning out these bins that hadn't been opened since the '20s or '30s, and I thought, 'well, I really shouldn't take the whole book.'"

These virtuosic Herriman originals, as well as the expressionistic pen-and-ink *Krazy Kat* panels might, nonetheless, explain the aspect of Gorey's work that is more modern than his nineteenth- and early twentieth-century forebears. Herriman used minimal backgrounds and broke through the traditional enclosed-panel structure. Likewise, rather than adhering to the Victorian illustrator's penchant for filling an image with excess lines and period tropes, Gorey focused his pen on making tightly rendered people, animals, and props, then silhouetting them against white or spare backgrounds. White space was an almost sanctified design element for modernist designers whose mission was to excise clutter from bourgeois taste. Gorey used chiaroscuro (the dynamic use of blacks and whites or lights and shades) for dramatic impact, his dark lines radiant against the empty backgrounds. He was not devoutly or even consciously a less-is-more adherent by any stretch, yet he did not reject it either. To see his original drawings, it is clear that precision was paramount: there was nothing extraneous, not an errant line or misplaced scribble. While every mark had its place, his drawings were never ham-fisted or stiff.

Another of Gorey's defining traits was his hand-lettered titles and subtitles for most of the book covers and jackets he designed. Diana Klemin, who began at Doubleday in 1945 and was Anchor's art director from 1953 to 1987, recalled in an interview with Mark Dery that Gorey's were hybrid typefaces "combining machine setting with calligraphy." Metal typesetting (later phototypesetting) was time-consuming and expensive in the 1950s, but Gorey was not just being frugal: "I didn't really know too much about type in those days, and it was simply easier to hand-letter the whole thing than to spec type. Eventually, though, I did a lot of things that weren't hand-lettered, as far as book jackets were concerned." Slightly rough versions of classical and neo-Gothic lettering traced from vintage type-specimen books became his trademark of sorts. For *Greek Tragedy: A Literary Study* by H. D. F. Kitto (p. 12) his lettering is indistinguishable from set type, whereas the title for *The Sot-Weed Factor* by John Barth (p. 13) is clearly hand-rendered, based on a nineteenth-century decorative Tuscan.

Gorey once sarcastically complained, "I was stuck with hand-lettering, which I did very poorly, I always felt—but everybody seemed to like it." He also did jobs and favors for other designers who "were even less competent in lettering than I was," he added.

When Gorey started writing and illustrating his own work, he said his friends suggested that he should use the hand-lettered style. "My first book was not hand-lettered, but my second one was, and after that there was no looking back." (A Gorey font was developed a number of years ago and is used on the cover of this very book.)

▪ ▪ ▪ ▪ ▪

Gorey was hesitant at first to move to New York City. He was actively engaged in the cultural life in Cambridge, Massachusetts, where he helped found the Poets' Theatre. But at Harvard (where he had roomed for a while with Frank O'Hara) he knew Jason Epstein and Barbara Zimmerman (later Epstein), who in 1953 cofounded the Anchor Books division of Doubleday. Gorey had graduated college in 1950, worked in a local bookstore, and tried to

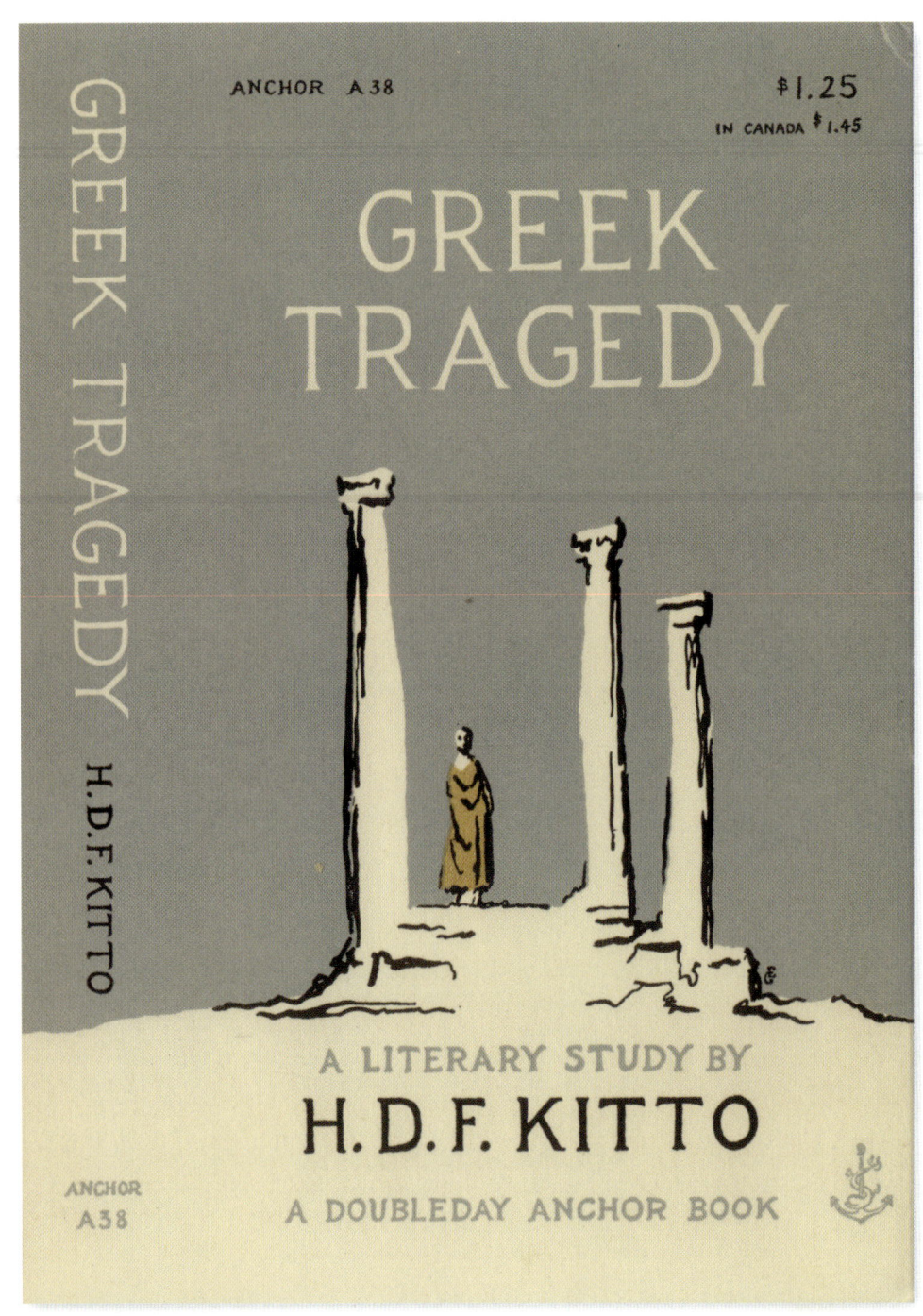

Greek Tragedy: A Literary Study by H. D. F. Kitto
Doubleday Anchor, 1954, PB

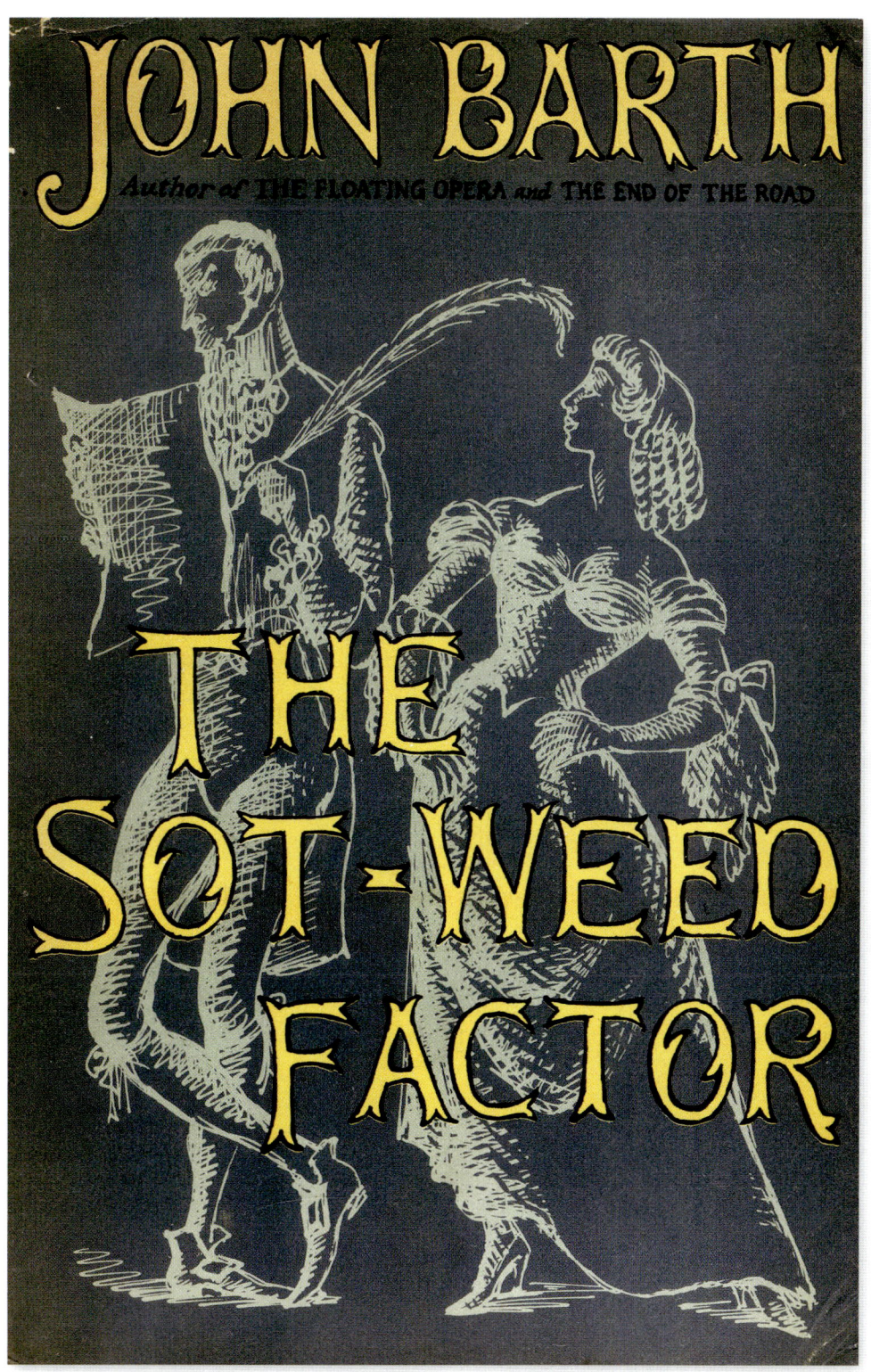

The Sot-Weed Factor by John Barth
Doubleday, 1960, HC

write a novel, which went nowhere. Epstein offered him a job, which Gorey initially turned down, but shortly later said, "I realized I was starving to death in Boston," and accepted. He had already made a few covers, then in 1953 he joined his friends as a Doubleday artist. Few artists were more suited for the job. Epstein and Zimmerman were well aware that Gorey devoured a regular diet of French symbolist and surrealist literature (which was his major at Harvard along with an interest in Chinese and Japanese literature) and was capable of getting to the meat of any text. "I was much better read than most of the people who were doing artwork," Gorey noted.

Gorey's first cover, *Lafcadio's Adventures* by André Gide, suggested his interest in classical drawing and late nineteenth-century cartoons. This has both going for it, plus a nod to Giorgio de Chirico. Yet it seems cluttered compared to later covers. The employ of extreme gesture in both the figures and the architecture makes this one of his more kinetic pieces. Gorey's second cover for a book, *Shakespeare* by Mark Van Doren (p. 16), was curiously less impressive and more staid than most others he did. Gorey described it as "a kind of tacky little drawing of the Globe Theatre from the air, which I found someplace and copied."

Like his contemporary cover artist colleagues, Gorey was not required to do a lot of preparation for the specific covers. "I was usually handed the assignment, and there would be some little paragraph summarizing the plot," he explained. In very many instances he already had read the book, sometimes more than once. But it rarely mattered anyway, since his style was so individual that the covers themselves did not literally illustrate scenes as much as they evoked moods or set off sparks of recognition.

Gorey was given certain authors to illustrate as a matter of course. He recalled, "I became very well known for my Henry James covers. I hate him more than anybody else in the world except for Picasso. . . . I've read everything of Henry James, some of it twice, and every time I do it I think, 'Why am I doing this again? Why am I torturing myself? I know how I feel. Why can't I just accept that?' . . . Everybody thought, 'Oh, how sensitive you are to Henry James,' and I thought, 'Oh sure, kids.' If it's because I hate him so much, that's probably true."

Epstein had a clear vision of the quintessential Anchor cover—and it included Gorey's artwork. In fact, Diana Klemin noted that Epstein wanted to see "the entire line as Gorey." But the sales people "hated" the idea of having more than four Goreyesque covers on one list. Nonetheless, "When he did a cover, you didn't have to say 'Change it.' He had an intuitive sense," Klemin said, adding, "He could have done the Sistine Chapel."

Gorey had a real knack for symbolic interpretation, but also a gift for "making the best color choices." Klemin recalled his ability to establish the right aura by using three flat colors plus black, what she called a "very refreshing use of color." For Franz Kafka's *Amerika* (p. 18), a novel about the American wanderings of Karl Roßmann, a 16-year-old exiled to New York because of a seduction scandal in Germany, the dominant color is a moody gray combined with subtle pink skylights, as though a touch of sun hit the bottom of a cloud. Gorey's color choice underscores his intention to suggest dislocation. The image is an ominous frieze of a lonely figure (Roßmann) on the deck of the ship while directly overhead, standing on the bridge, is the captain looking through a telescope at the ghostly city skyline. The two Goreyesque characters are frozen in anticipation of what awaits. It is hard not to experience the emotional power projected through this

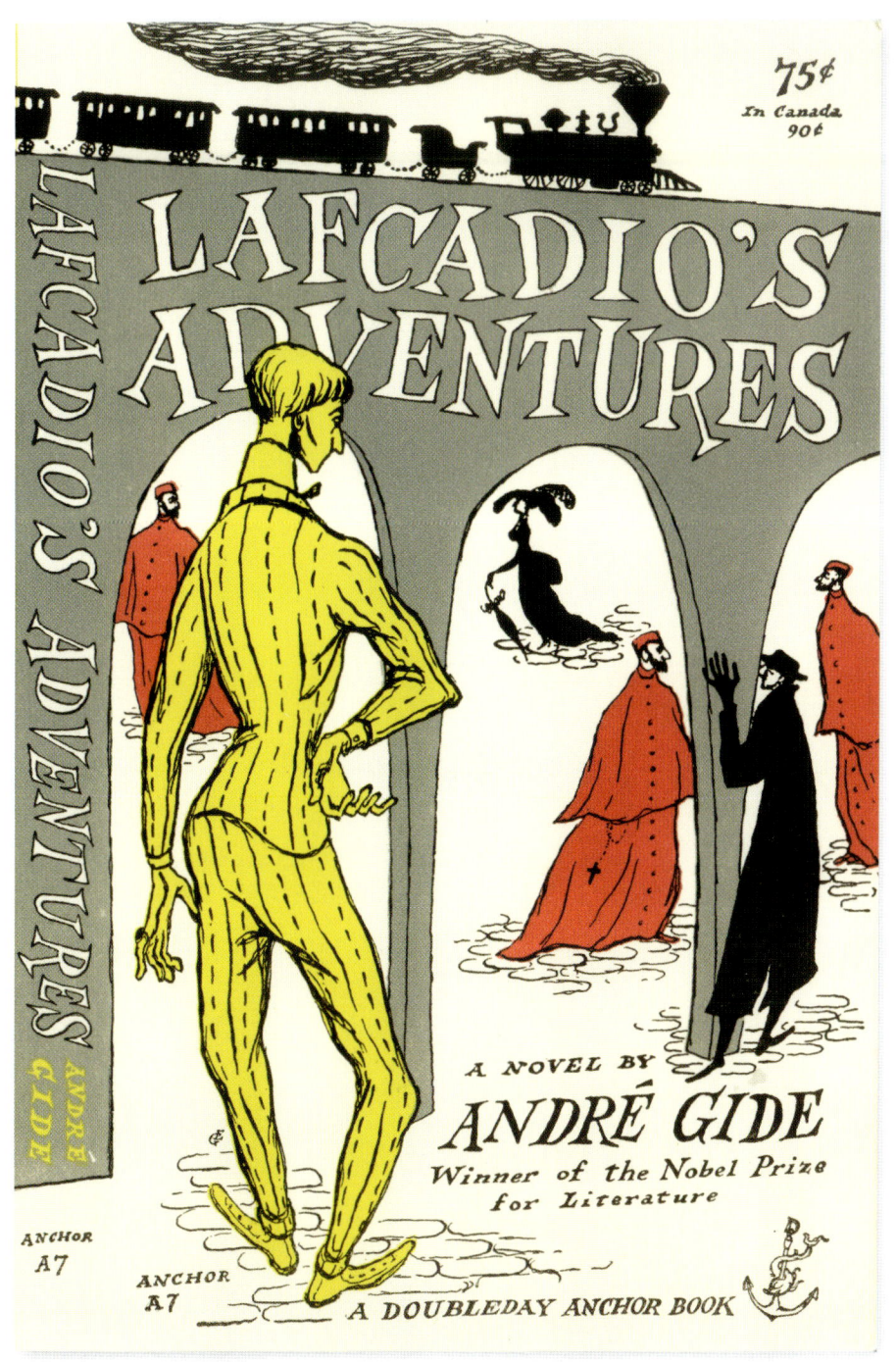

Lafcadio's Adventures by André Gide
Doubleday Anchor, 1953, PB

Shakespeare by Mark Van Doren
Doubleday Anchor, 1953, PB

cover—this intense blast of existential loss and future discovery is every bit as striking today as when published in 1955.

Flat color-printing inks for Gorey are like the melodramatic extremes of light and dark for the noir cinematographer. The deliberate choice of hue is both design tool and dramatic device and is used to focus the viewer's eyes on a character. Color heightens anxiety in Gorey's cover for François Mauriac's *Thérèse* (p. 19), about a woman who has poisoned her husband and reflects on her reasons, spending the novel recalling her deed. It is dominated by two shades of sienna, one for the ground, the other the sky. The viewer's eye, however, is directed to a crimson hat and coat on a woman sitting joylessly (or maybe not) alone on a small bench with her thoughts. Color washes over the minimally expressive line work and imposes a sense of sorrow over the entire vignette. The viewer is encouraged to question what came before and comes after this frozen moment. Curiously, more recent covers for the same novel show a painting or photograph of a disingenuously anguished face in an overt representation of Thérèse, a theatrical movie version of the character. Conversely, Gorey routinely restrained himself from the tired cliché—doing the obvious was his bugaboo. What he did so well with this, and most of his covers and jacket illustrations, was leave traces of ambiguity, sometimes through his use of light and gesture, which left room for individual interpretation. It was as if Gorey were subliminally encouraging the viewer to interact with the picture. This freedom to interpret (and solve the mystery of) his pictures *and* words is the special pleasure found in Gorey's work.

There is, moreover, consensual intimacy between Gorey and reader, beyond the license of interpretation. A few covers, including *Pleasures and Days* by Marcel Proust (p. 46), *The Autobiography of William Butler Yeats* (p. 55), and *The Garden to the Sea* by Philip Toynbee (p. 35), project a generic quality, as though anyone could have done them, and appear to block the reader out. Yet the vast majority of Gorey's cover work engages and invites the reader to join some primal level of recognition. Whether it is the acerbic humor of Anton Chekhov's *St. Peter's Day* (p. 59), with the commentary on the Edwardian bird shooters and birds falling from the sky, or Henry James's *What Maisie Knew* (p. 20), with the ghostly little Maisie watching her worried parents, the connection resides in empathy. Readers are certainly drawn to these covers for their artistry and wit, but find there is more resonance in the heart of Gorey's pictorial voice.

Having to use three flat colors plus black, rather than process color, was the factor that would give his paperback covers a certain silkscreened or etched look. Using matte cover stock ensured a subdued outcome. "I guess I could have picked bright reds or blues, but I've never been much for that," Gorey noted when asked about his rationale. "My palette seems to be sort of lavender, lemon yellow, olive green, and then a whole series of absolutely no colors at all." As his own novels, storybooks, and illustrations evidence, he was virtuosic with black and white, which carried through on his own books and those where he controlled the cover and interior design. One of the most exquisite (and modern) designs is the cover of Edward Lear's *The Dong with a Luminous Nose* (p. 89), a one-color-plus-black composition where he used rays of white light to make the reader ponder over that luminous nose. The spareness of these covers belies what is arguably some of Gorey's most intricate line work inside.

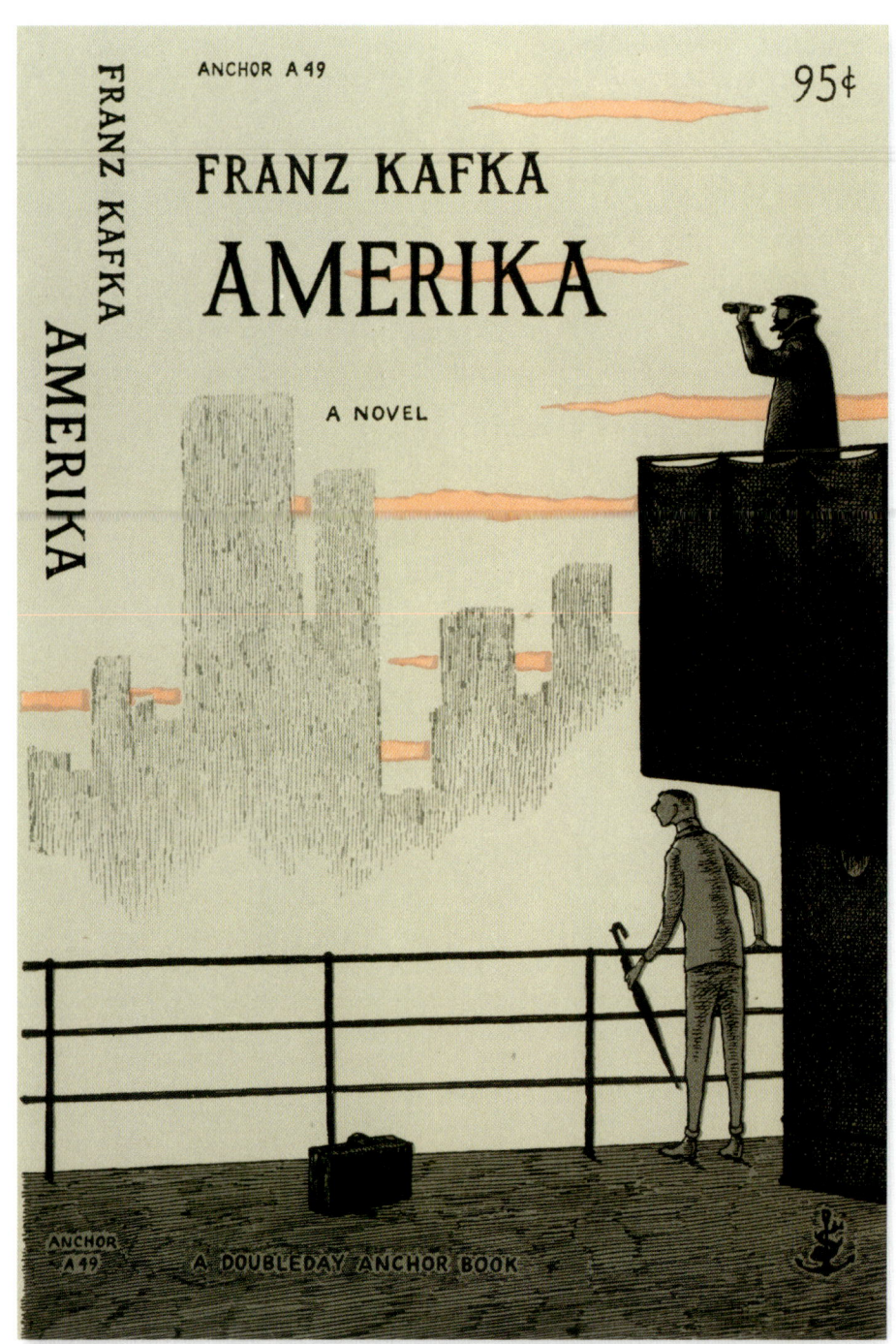

Amerika by Franz Kafka
Doubleday Anchor, 1955, PB

Thèrése by François Mauriac
Doubleday Anchor, 1956, PB, text illus.

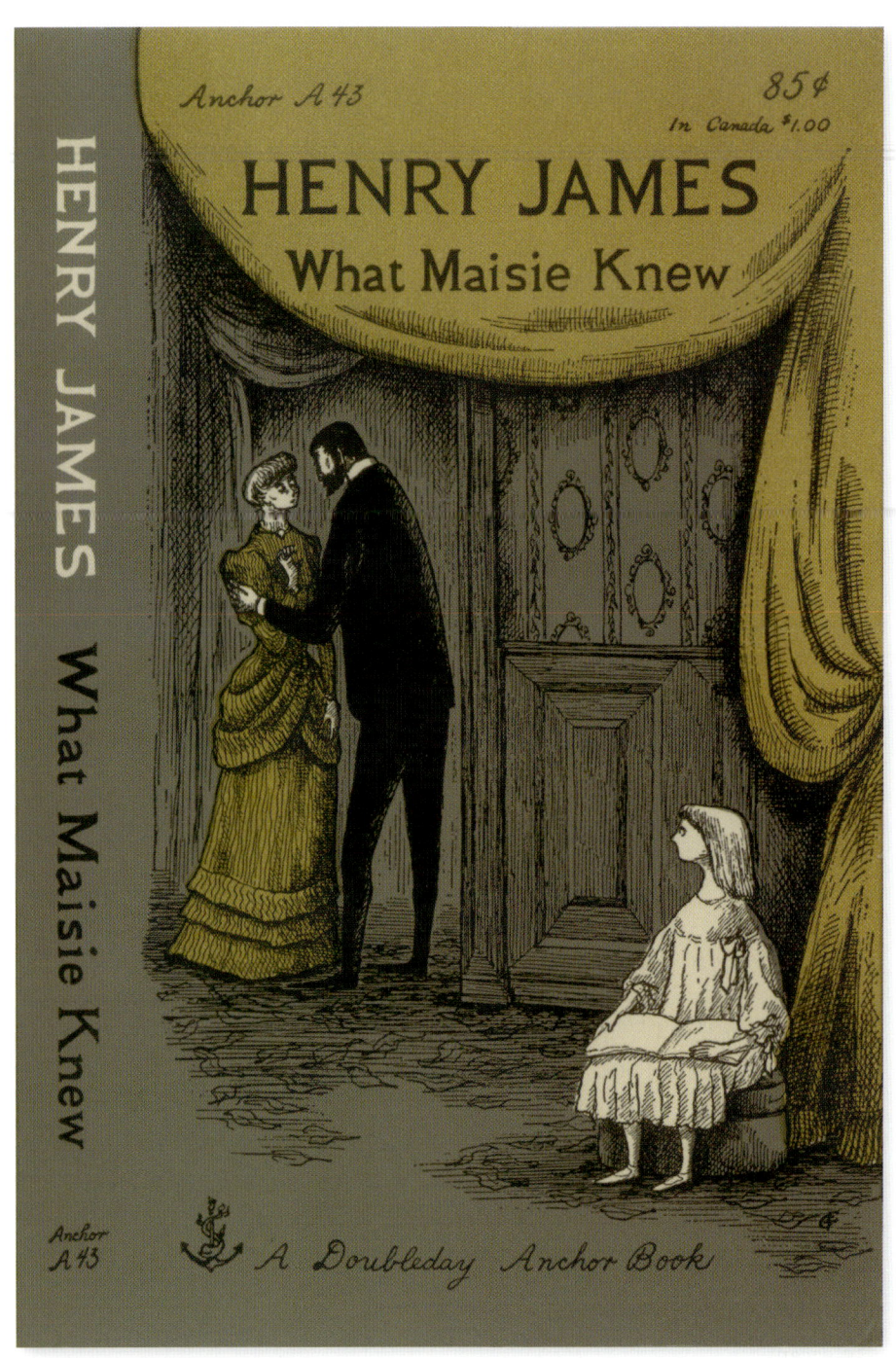

What Maisie Knew by Henry James
Doubleday Anchor, 1954, PB

Given the usually short time involved in conceiving and producing the mechanicals for a cover, Gorey admittedly followed certain self-imposed routines, "such as my famous landscape which was mostly sky so I could fit in a title. Things like *The American Puritans*, *Victory* by Joseph Conrad, and *The Wanderer* tend to have low-lying landscapes, a lot of sky, sort of odd colors, and tiny figures that I didn't have to draw very hard." His references were varied. For the cover of *A Hero of Our Time* by Mihail Lermontov (p. 22), an awesome yet simple composition showing a vast sky and high mountains with little figures on horses, Gorey modestly quipped, "I assure you that was taken from some painting, maybe by Lermontov himself."

Despite Gorey's occasional self-deprecations regarding his covers and jackets, authors were usually very pleased with his interpretations. Whether or not he followed "routines," he had a keen ability to use his tropes in unusual ways. Such is the case with the jacket for Eliot's *Old Possum's Book*: the "practical cats" pose on an architectural monument that provides armature for his lettering, for which Gorey borrowed the baroque design practice of using headstones, vases, and drapes (among other flourishes) as framing devices. He did a few text-only covers and jackets, including Søren Kierkegaard's *Either/Or*, one that "I just did tacky hand-lettering for." Gorey described the rationale for this image-free cover in his sardonic way: "Was I planning to sit down and read Kierkegaard at that point? No, I wasn't! And it wouldn't have helped if I had, I'm sure. I probably would have been completely paralyzed. That was the kind of thing where they just wanted lettering."

But don't be fooled. Gorey did not routinely give them what they wanted. His images followed his own logic and understanding.

By his own admission, Gorey's job in Anchor's art department, located in a crowded single room in New York's Time & Life Building, was never too taxing. "In fact, when I saw some of the paste-ups that other people did, I thought that these well-known artists [such as Ben Shahn and others who also did Doubleday covers] really were all thumbs," he said. "I never had much patience with having to redo other people's paste-ups, which looked like they'd just flung the lettering on the page."

In 1953, Gorey published his first book, *The Unstrung Harp* with Duell, Sloan and Pearce, which had just merged with Little, Brown. It is what Graham Greene called "the best novel ever written about a novelist, and I ought to know." It was unique in its vintageness, particularly at that historical moment when abstract expressionism was influencing so many artists and designers. At the same time, however, conventional American magazine and book illustrators of the *Saturday Evening Post* school were entrenched in realism and more representational than ever. It is a sixty-four-page tale seductively drawn in a crypto-Edwardian manner, concerning the trials and tribulations of the fictional author Clavius Frederick Earbrass, a struggling novelist in a lush fur coat who lives alone in a stately house full of portraits and statuettes that look exactly like him. Gorey's imaginary tableaux are replete with turn-of-the-century trappings (velvet drapes, marble mantelpieces, four-poster beds, ornate urns, vases of aspidistras, a Fantod under a bell jar) and inhabited with eccentric and sinister personae: gents and dames.

Furthermore, as other books emerged, Gorey's repertory contained a menagerie of hippos, birds, alligators, bats, and cats. Through enigmatic crosshatched drawings and

A Hero of Our Time by Mihail Lermontov
Doubleday Anchor, 1956, PB

staccato narrative rhythms, Gorey created a world that transcended time and place, where even the unspeakable is occasionally spoken, the unthinkable is thought, and murder and mayhem can be sinfully comic. It left his readers with what Dale Roylance, then curator of the Arts of the Book Collection at Yale University, called "mixed feelings of amusement and uneasiness," adding, "Few artists since Grandville and Edward Lear have created more engagingly demented illustrated books."

1953 was also the year Gorey started at Anchor. During the next few years, as the *New York Times* obituary stated, he worked on his own books while at Anchor, publishing *The Listing Attic* (Duell, Sloan and Pearce / Little, Brown) in 1954, *The Doubtful Guest* (Doubleday) in 1957, and *The Object-Lesson* (Doubleday) in 1958. The next year, 1959, Gorey's work attracted the attention of *New Yorker* literary critic Edmund Wilson, who praised his books as "surrealistic and macabre, amusing and somber, nostalgic and claustrophobic, poetic and poisoned."

With this stunning notice by one of the world's great critics it might appear that Gorey earned his Get Out of Jail Free card to leave the publishing art departments for a larger stage. But 1959 to 1960 was also the period that Jason Epstein had started a publishing venture called Looking Glass Library with Clelia Carroll at Random House. He pressed Gorey into service as editor with W. H. Auden and Edmund Wilson. "The idea was to do for children's books what Anchor had done for the parents," Gorey recalled about the plan to publish classic children's books. The books were not paperbacks, but rather paper-over-boards, and by Gorey's standard, "It was really quite a good series." He nonetheless added, "Well, the paper was perfectly dreadful, but then the paper for everything in those days was perfectly terrible."

Gorey illustrated a few books in the series ("The less said about those, the better," he said). He was also the art director and an ersatz editor "in a sense, because I helped pick some of the books." They produced three of Andrew Lang's colored *Fairy* books and a wonderful anthology of poetry for children by Janet Adams Smith that started at Faber in England. There was something called *The Comic Looking Glass* (p. 24). Richard Hughes did a book of children's stories called *The Spider's Palace*. Then there was Charlotte M. Yonge's *Countess Kate*. "It was really a neat batch of sometimes quite forgotten nineteenth-century stories from England." Gorey also created the jacket for H. G. Wells's *War of The Worlds* (pp. 26–27), a slight detour from his developing style, looking more like a comic strip panel than a Goreyesque vignette. He enjoyed the process of making sophisticated children's books and thought it "was really a good idea," he noted, "but then Jason lost interest, and after two years the whole thing folded up."

Gorey did freelance work for Grosset & Dunlap and Vintage Books, which was famous for using the cream of mid-century modern designers. In 1961, Nobel laureate Hermann Hesse recommended Gorey's work to his Swiss German-language publisher, Diogenes Verlag. Today, Gorey's works have been translated into seventeen foreign languages. For one year, 1963, Gorey was the art director at Bobbs-Merrill, which the staff referred to with the Goreyism "Boobs Muddle." "Eventually there was internecine warfare, and I was unfortunately on the side of the president, who got fired with all his entourage," he recalled. "Which was just as well. After that I just had too much freelance work to look for another job, and I moved up to the Cape for the summers."

The Comic Looking Glass edited by Hart Day Leavitt
Looking Glass Library, 1961, HC, text illus.

At this juncture, 1964, Gorey decided to venture into what Gotham Book Mart's Andreas Brown calls the "abyss"—or what Gorey called becoming a freelance illustrator and book designer. He even designed a business card (title page), which Brown, who was an early Gorey enthusiast, publisher, and friend, does not believe was ever printed. It features two of Gorey's 1964 *Nursery Frieze* baby hippos with "Book Design" and "Edward Gorey" word ribbons coming from their heads and lists his 36 East 38th Street address and telephone number.

The next phase of his professional life was devoted to books and storytelling. He jumped into the children's book field as well. But like the works of his fellow illustrators Tomi Ungerer and R. O. Blechman, who were also doing visual storybooks alternately for adults and children, the stories and humor were decidedly more sophisticated than the standard kiddy fare. That, however, did not stop Gorey from teaching a class called Advanced Children's Book Illustration at New York's School of Visual Arts for three years starting in 1965 (by then he had "written and illustrated 17 books, both for adults and children"). The course was announced in a brochure smartly designed to resemble a book jacket (pp. 28–29), with a cover illustration of the back of a man—Gorey?—crouching on yet another baby hippo and wearing a wide-brim straw hat with a listless bird atop it.

The description of his course dryly sums up Gorey's life in the commercial arts: "The course will emphasize the creative and imaginative aspects of illustrating—and writing—children's books and give practical experience in techniques, media, design, and typography. . . . The main work of the course will be illustrating and designing a complete book."

Gorey went on to write and illustrate a slew of books, and he illustrated texts for other authors, from Samuel Beckett to John Updike. His ancillaries, including toys, posters, pop-ups, miniature books, and many magazine and newspaper appearances, grew significantly. He made an absurd alphabet book, *Figbash Acrobate* published by his Fantod Press (1994), in which a ballet of his reptilian creatures form letters. A catalog published by Gotham Book Mart & Gallery Inc. from Fall/Winter 1976 lists more than 210 items for sale—just a tip of the Gorey iceberg. Maybe it is a portion of a Gorey glacier that partly obscured his significant cover and jacket output. Gorey continued to do covers for his own books, notably the *Amphigorey* series, as well as various others, represented here.

A few years before his passing, Gorey suggested to me in an interview that his covers and jackets were as much a part of his creative grand plan—the building of an interconnected oeuvre—as any other of his more authorial métiers. Demonstrating his indefatigable willingness, Gorey added, "I still do book jacket work occasionally, if somebody calls me up."

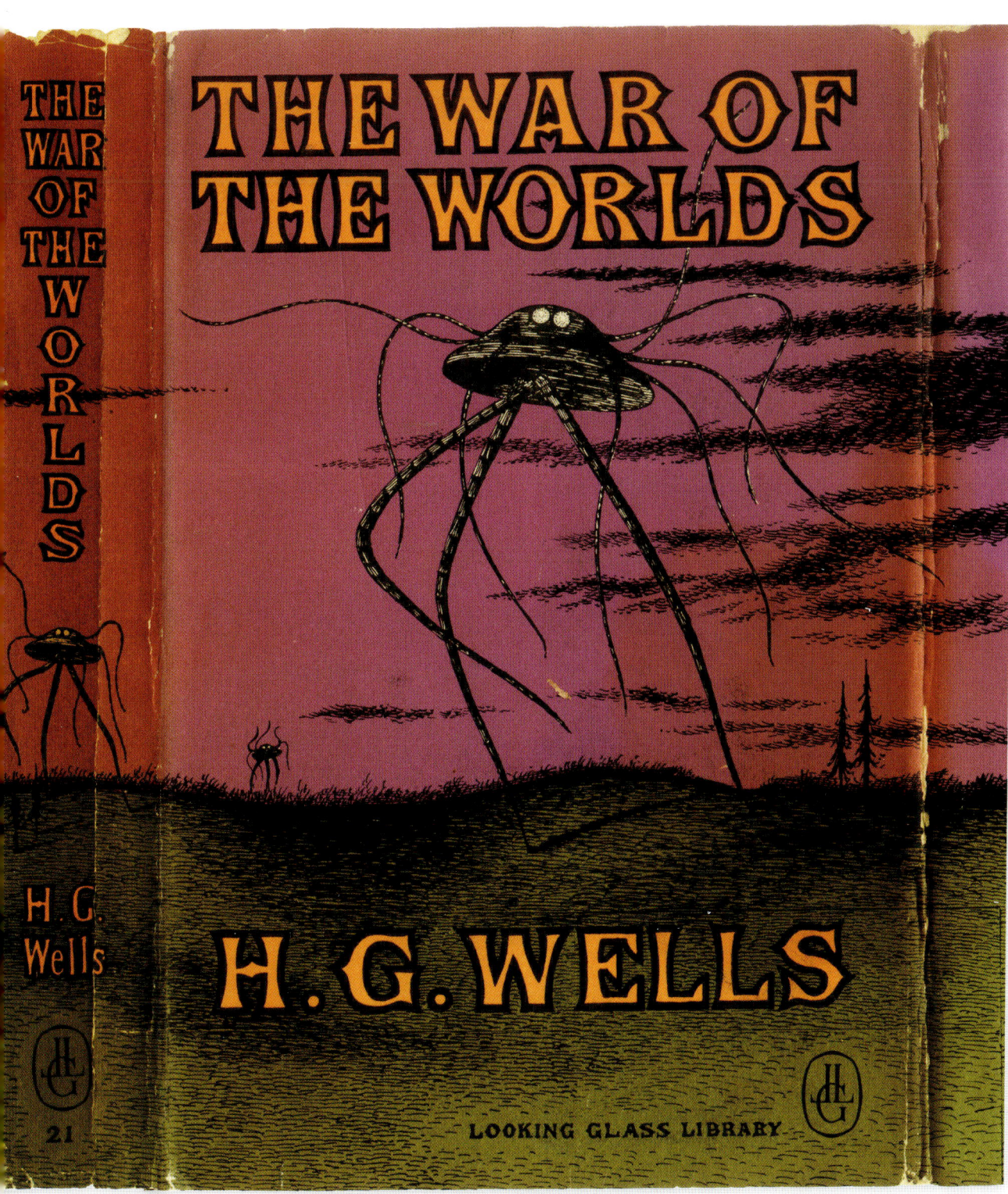

The War of the Worlds by H. G. Wells
Looking Glass Library, 1960, HC, text illus.

(Continued from front flap)

with the nature of illustration, its various kinds and purposes, its relationship to text, and the two conceived as an entity. It will attempt to cover as many concepts, approaches, sources as possible to help the student develop his own talents and ideas in the field. Short assignments on specific problems which may be added to the student's portfolio will be given throughout the course. The main work of the course will be illustrating and designing a complete book.

Instructor: Edward Gorey Born Chicago 1925, graduated from Harvard 1950. With Doubleday from 1953 to 1960 as artist and typographer. Art director and editor with Looking Glass Library, 1960-2. Since then free-lance illustrator and book designer. Edward Gorey has written and illustrated 17 books, both for adults and children, the most recent being *The Sinking Spell* and *The Remembered Visit*.

Wednesday evenings, 6:40 to 9:40 P.M. Course begins September 22, 1965. Inquire: Office of Admissions, School of Visual Arts, 209 E. 23rd St., New York, N.Y. 10010. OR 9-7350

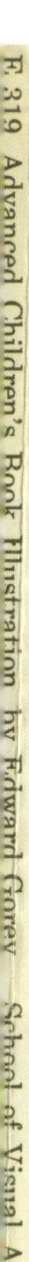

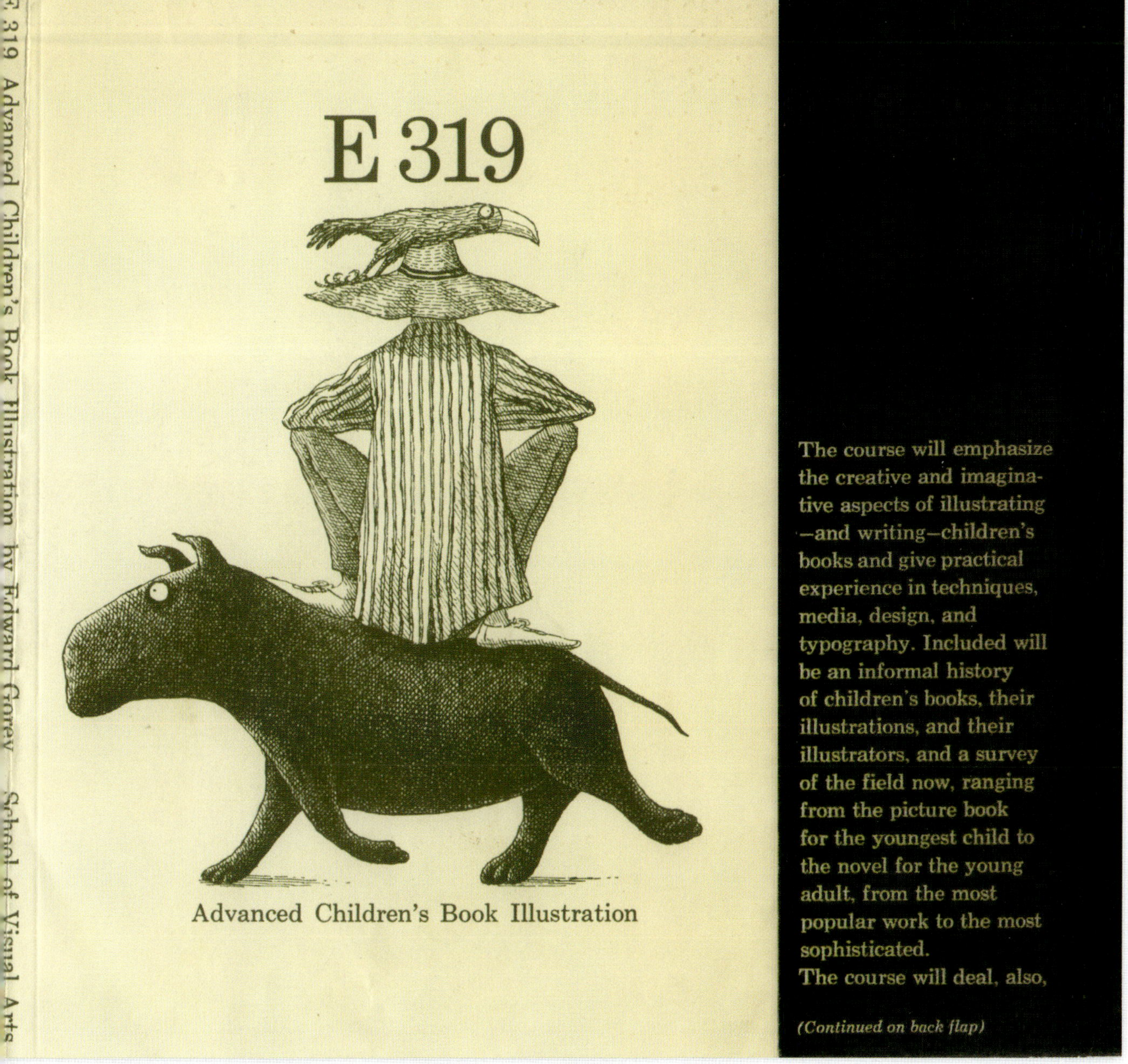
E 319 Advanced Children's Book Illustration by Edward Gorey School of Visual Arts
E 319
Advanced Children's Book Illustration
The course will emphasize the creative and imaginative aspects of illustrating —and writing—children's books and give practical experience in techniques, media, design, and typography. Included will be an informal history of children's books, their illustrations, and their illustrators, and a survey of the field now, ranging from the picture book for the youngest child to the novel for the young adult, from the most popular work to the most sophisticated.
The course will deal, also,
(Continued on back flap)

Advanced Children's Book Illustration course brochure, 1965

Bleak House by Charles Dickens
Doubleday, 1953, HC, text illus.

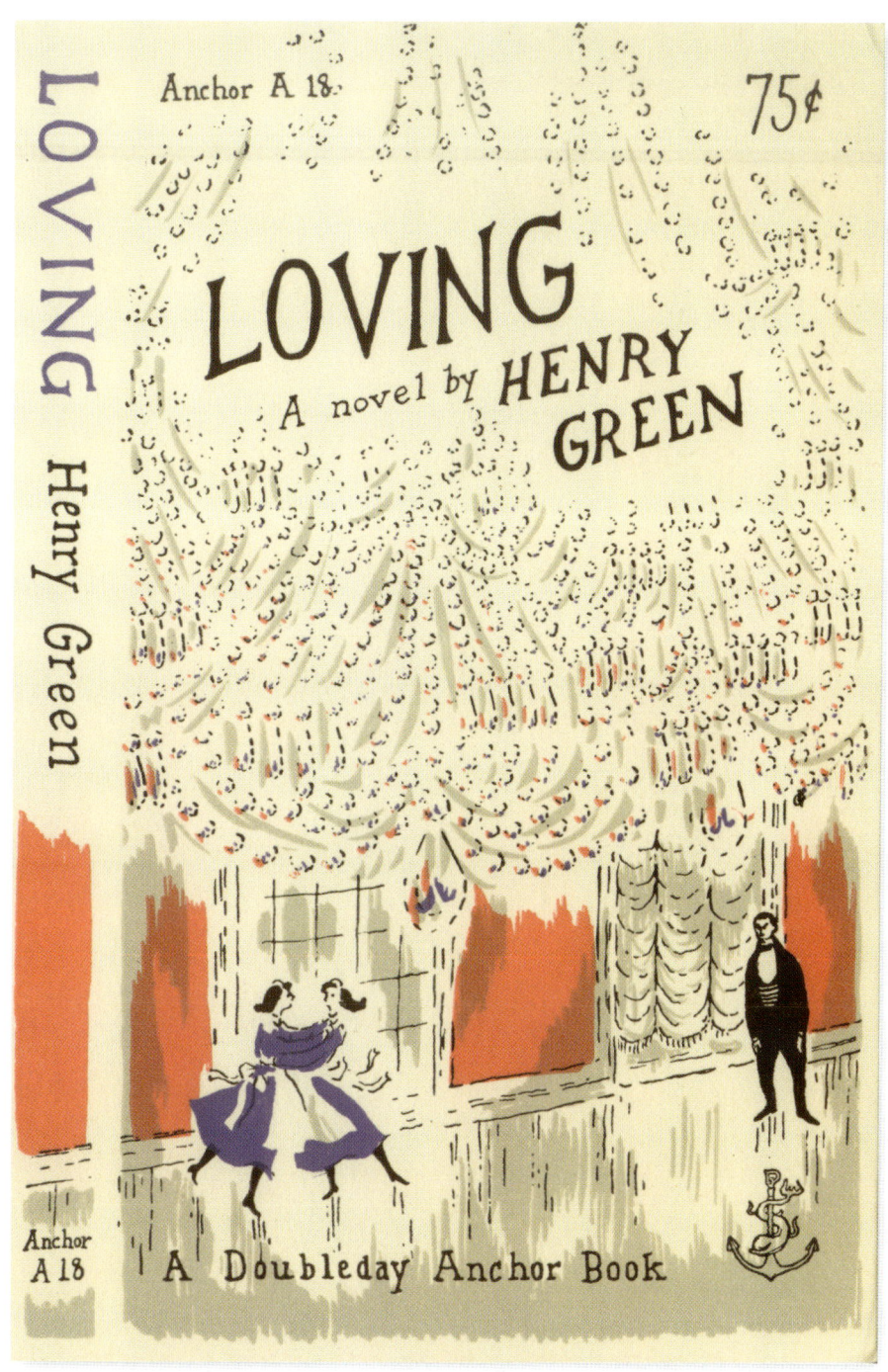

Loving by Henry Green
Doubleday Anchor, 1953, PB

The Romance of Tristan and Iseult by Joseph Bédier
Doubleday Anchor, 1953, PB

The Secret Agent by Joseph Conrad
Doubleday Anchor, 1953, PB

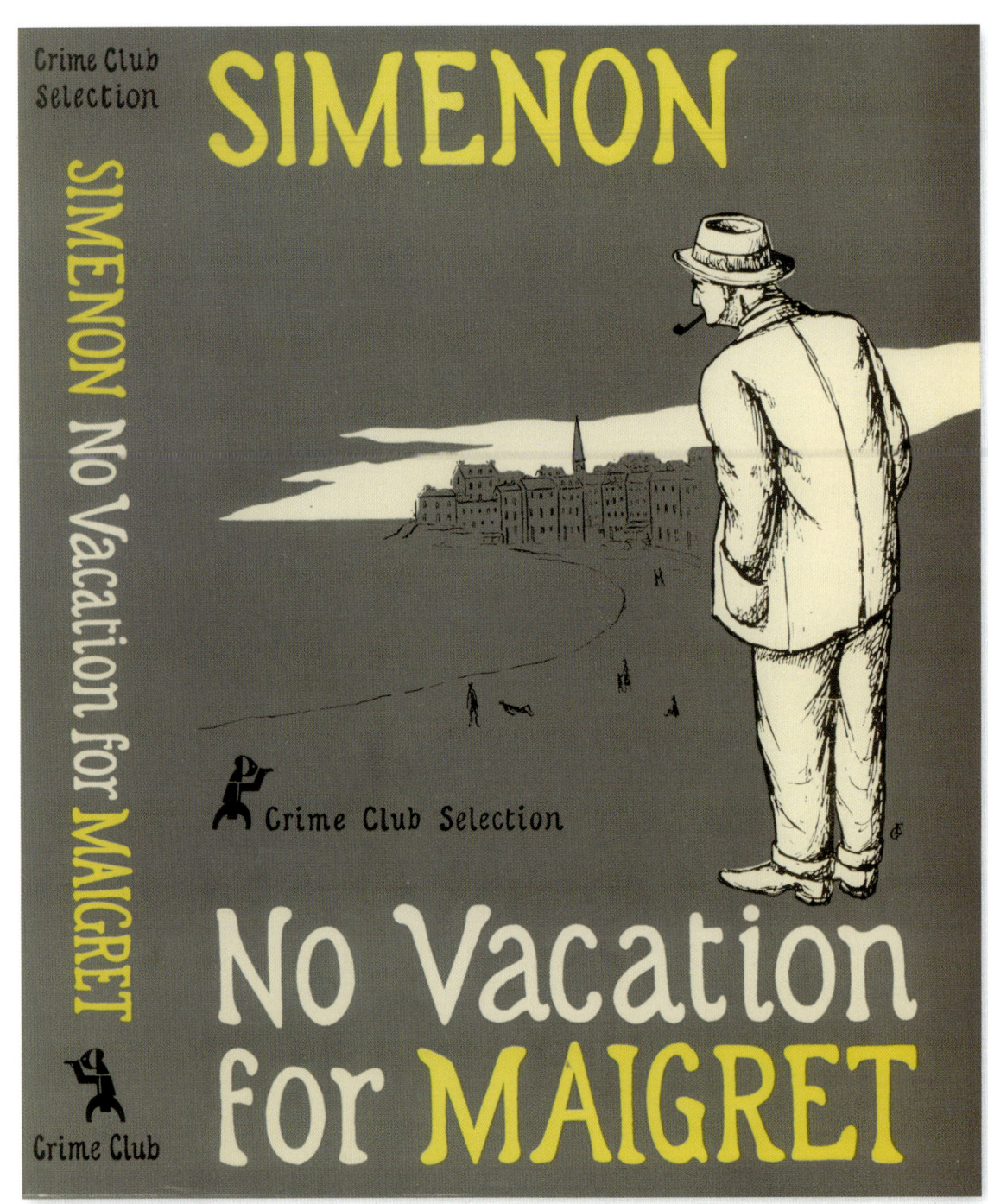

No Vacation for Maigret by Georges Simenon
Doubleday (Crime Club), 1953, HC

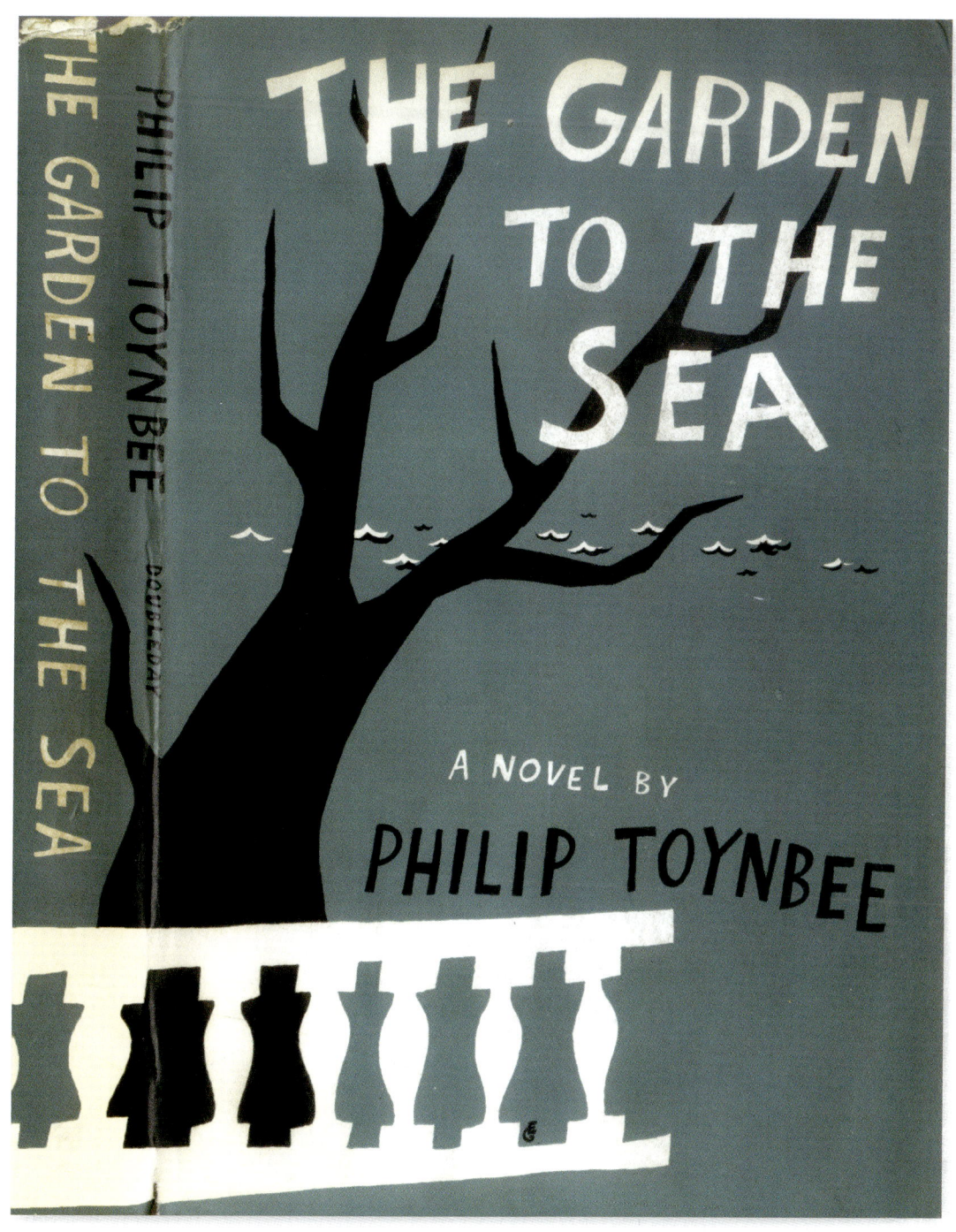

The Garden to the Sea by Philip Toynbee
Doubleday, 1954, HC

It Isn't This Time of Year at All! An Unpremeditated Autobiography by Oliver St. John Gogarty
Doubleday, 1954, HC

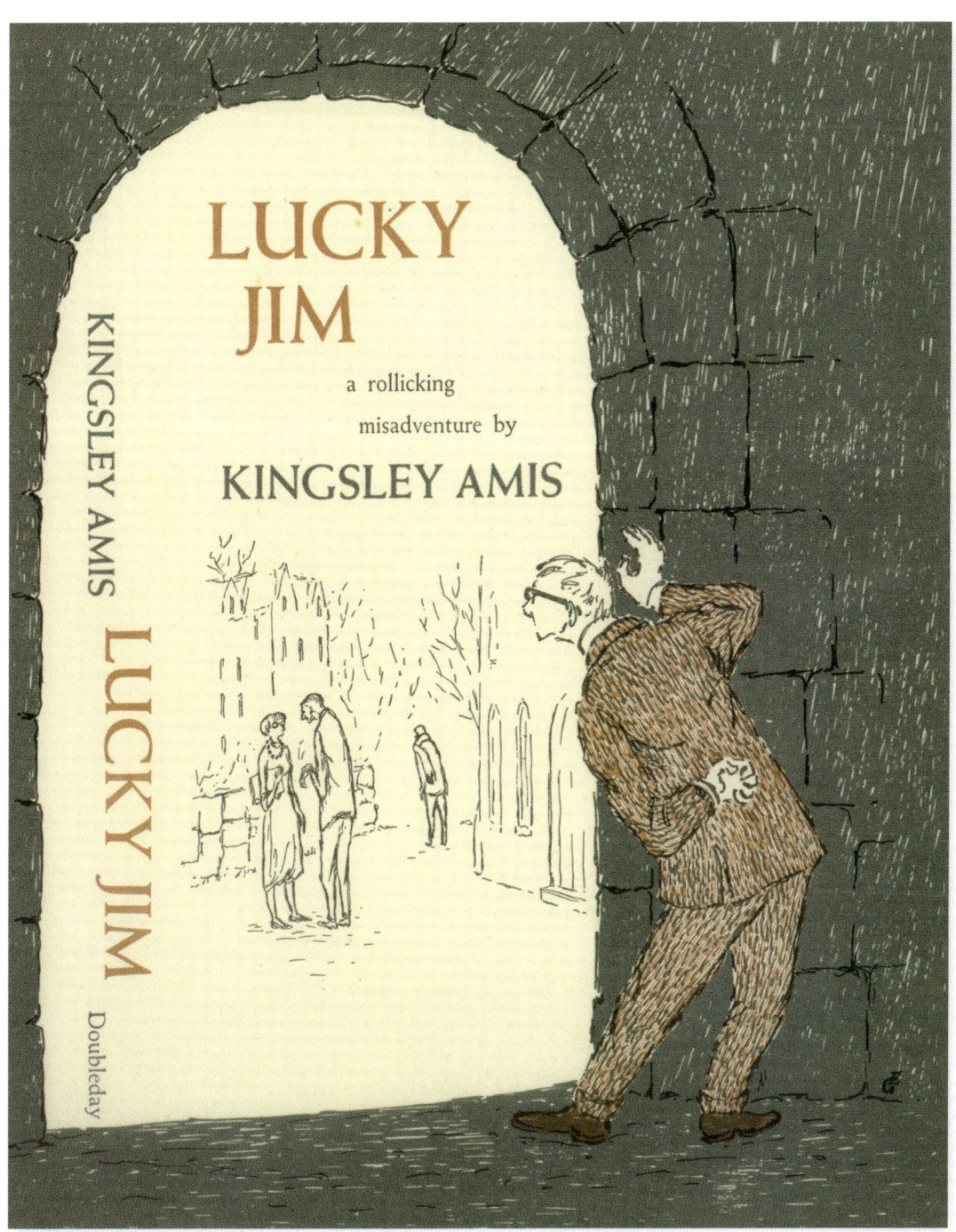

Lucky Jim by Kingsley Amis
Doubleday, 1954, HC

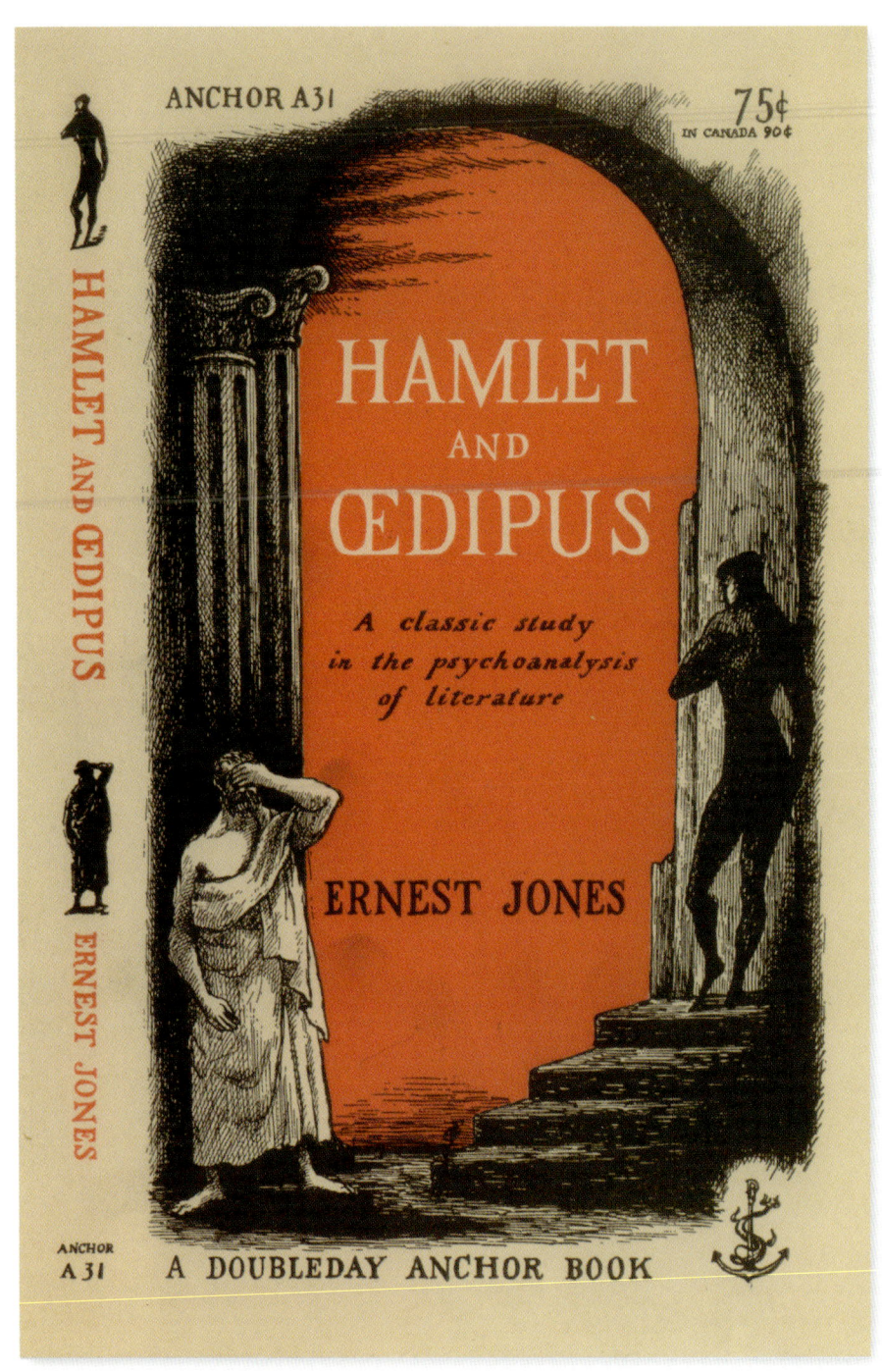

Hamlet and Oedipus: A Classic Study in the Psychoanalysis of Literature by Ernest Jones
Doubleday Anchor, 1954, PB

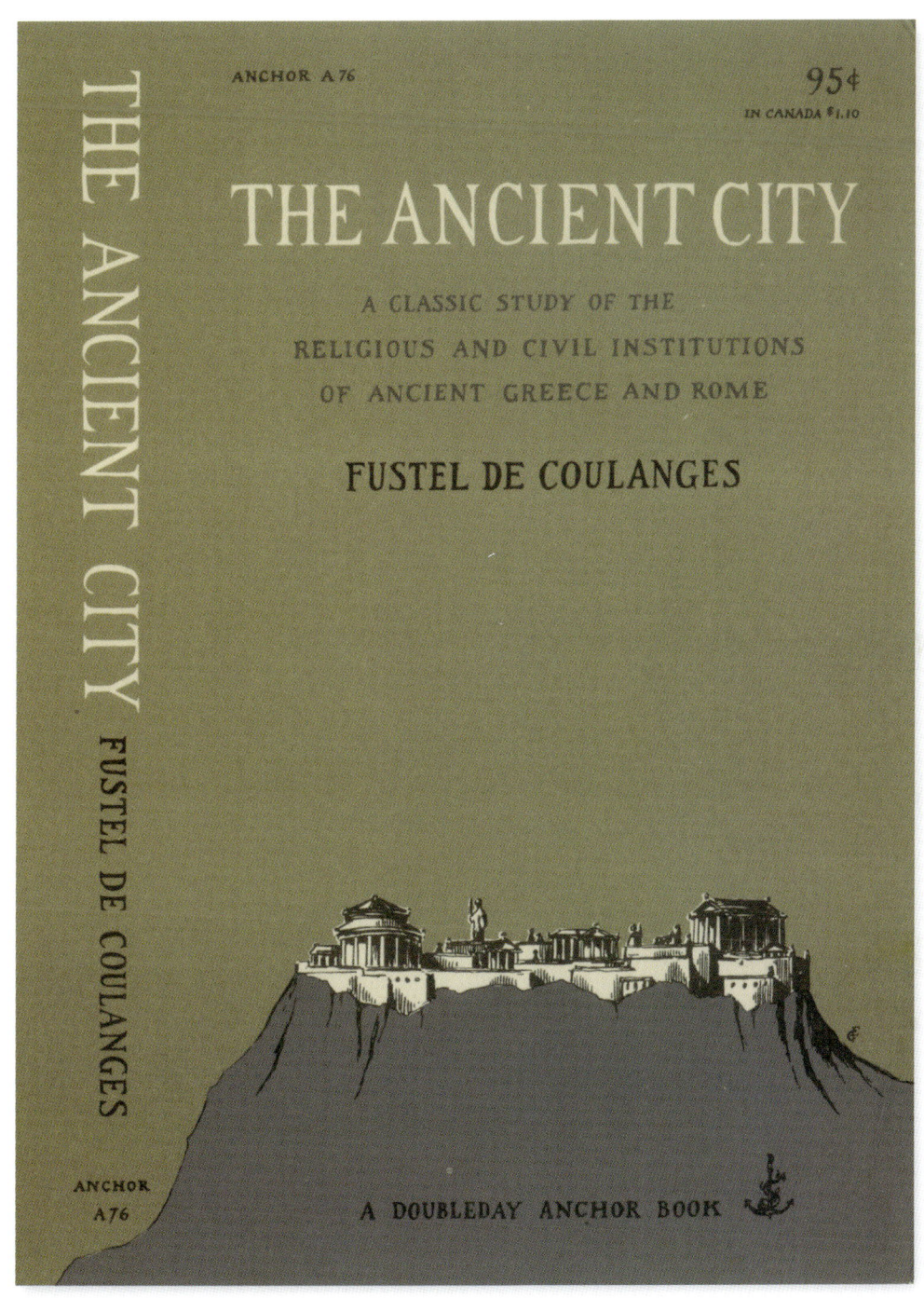

The Ancient City: A Classic Study of the Religious and Civil Institutions of Ancient Greece and Rome by Numa Denis Fustel De Coulanges
Doubleday Anchor, 1955, PB

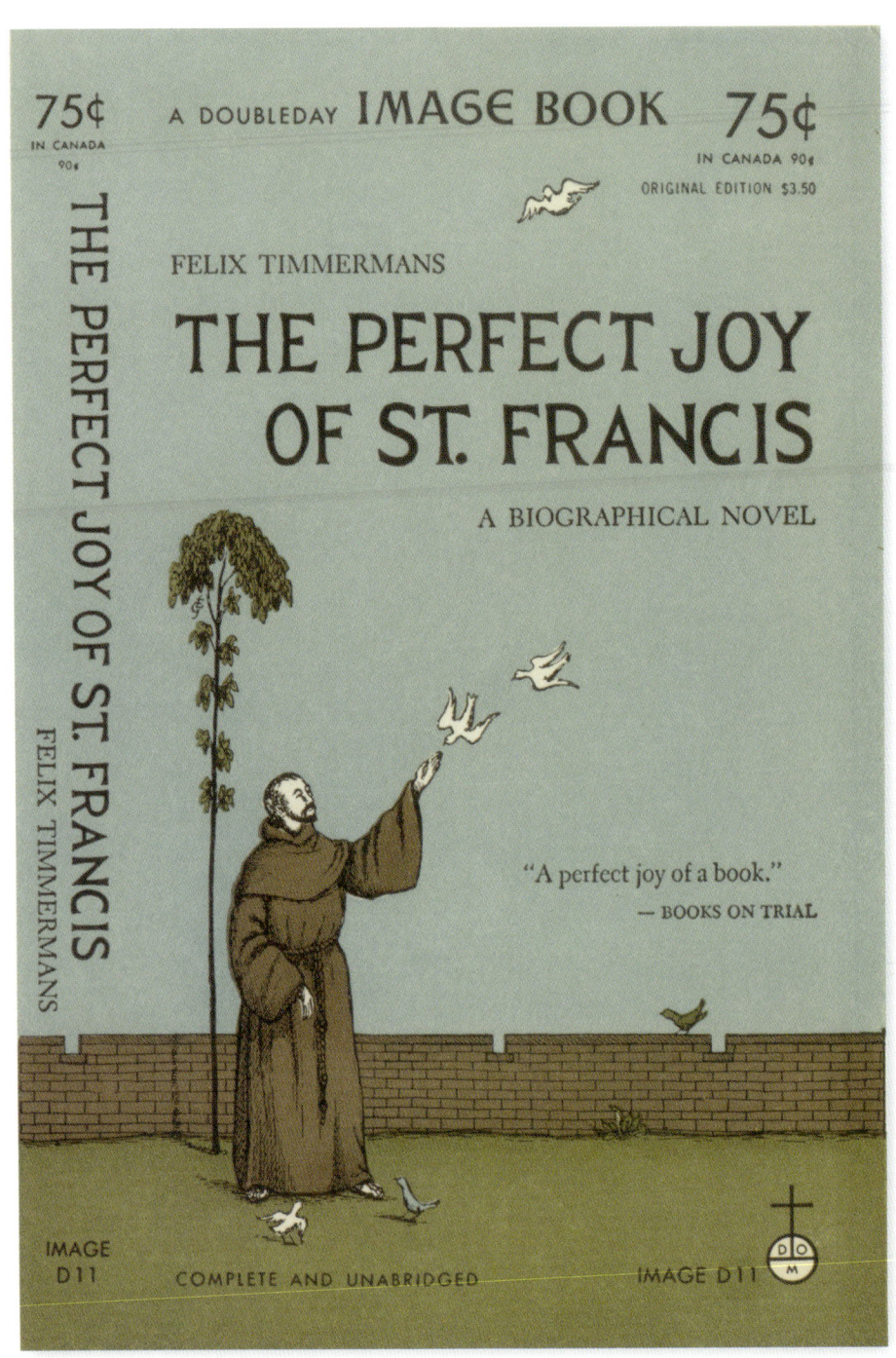

The Perfect Joy of St. Francis by Felix Timmermans
Doubleday Image, 1955, PB

Start from Somewhere Else: An Exposition of Wit and Humor Polite and Perilous by Oliver St. John Gogarty
Doubleday, 1955, HC

AN ELIZABETHAN SONG BOOK

The Elizabethan age and the years immediately after the death of Queen Elizabeth were the great age of English song. Poets like Shakespeare, Ben Jonson, John Donne and Thomas Campian wrote directly for composers of song; and great composers like John Dowland, Thomas Morley and Thomas Campian set their poems to music. The words and music are both here — the accompaniments, originally written for the lute, have been arranged for the piano by Noah Greenberg, director of the Pro Musica Antiqua of New York. The eighty-four songs have been selected by W. H. Auden, Mr. Greenberg and Chester Kallman, for both their words and music, and the perfection with which the two are brought together. Mr. Auden and Mr. Greenberg have also supplied full introductions on the words and music.

Here is a rare feast for lovers of English poetry and English song. For the first time, some of the most exquisite moments in the history of poetry and song can be recaptured by the general reader and amateur musician.

A DOUBLEDAY ANCHOR BOOK

An Elizabethan Song Book: Lute Songs; Madrigals & Rounds edited by Noah Greenberg, W. H. Auden, and Chester Kallman
Doubleday Anchor, 1955, PB

The Web and the Rock by Thomas Wolfe
Grossett & Dunlap (Universal Library), c. 1950s, HC

You Can't Go Home Again by Thomas Wolfe
Grosset & Dunlap (Universal Library), c. 1950s, HC

Pleasures and Days and Other Writings by Marcel Proust
Doubleday Anchor, 1957, PB

The Middle of the Journey by Lionel Trilling
Doubleday Anchor, 1957, PB, text illus.

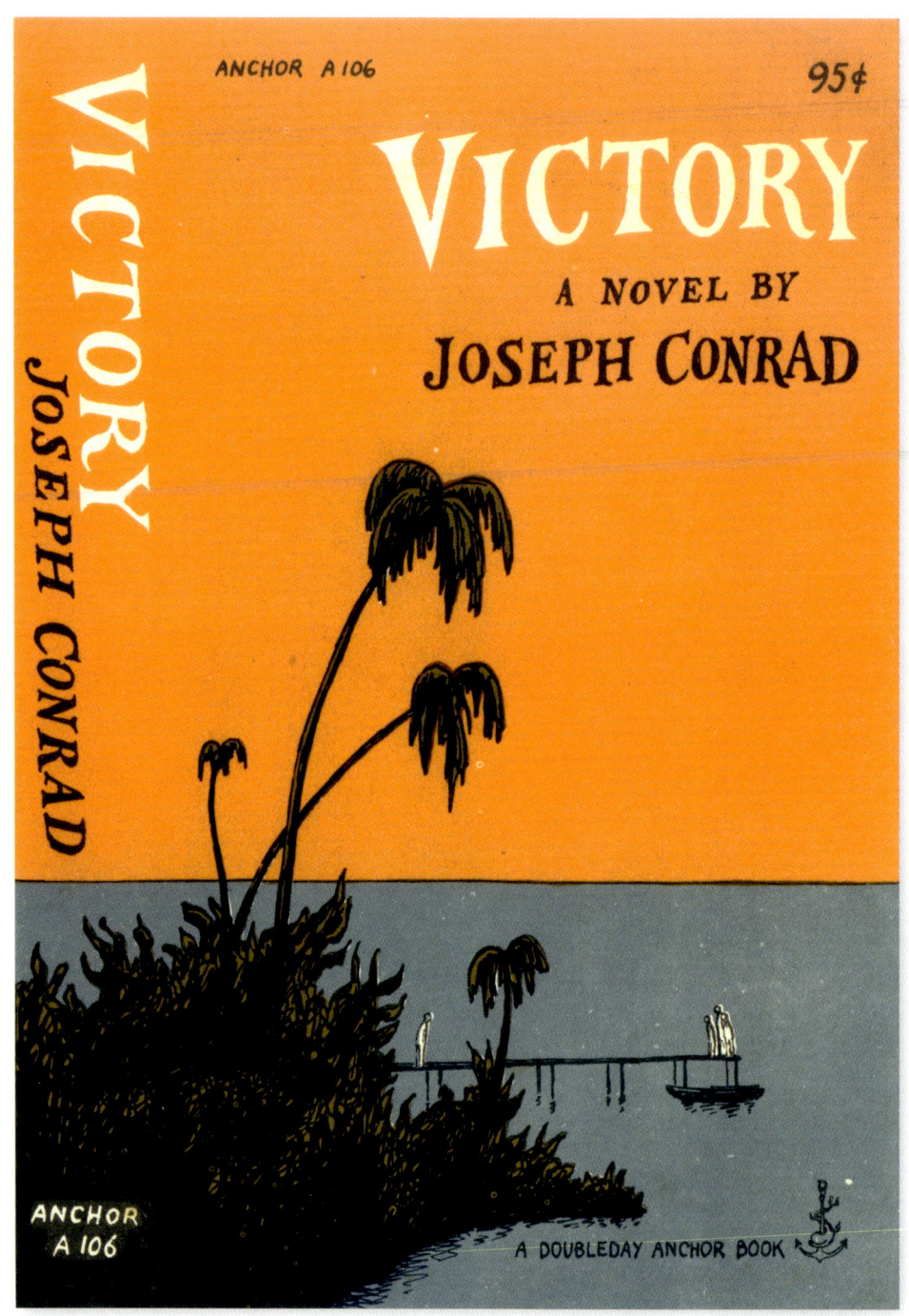

Victory by Joseph Conrad
Doubleday Anchor, 1957, PB, text illus.

Chance by Joseph Conrad
Doubleday Anchor, 1957, PB

Stendhal: On Love
Doubleday Anchor, 1957, PB

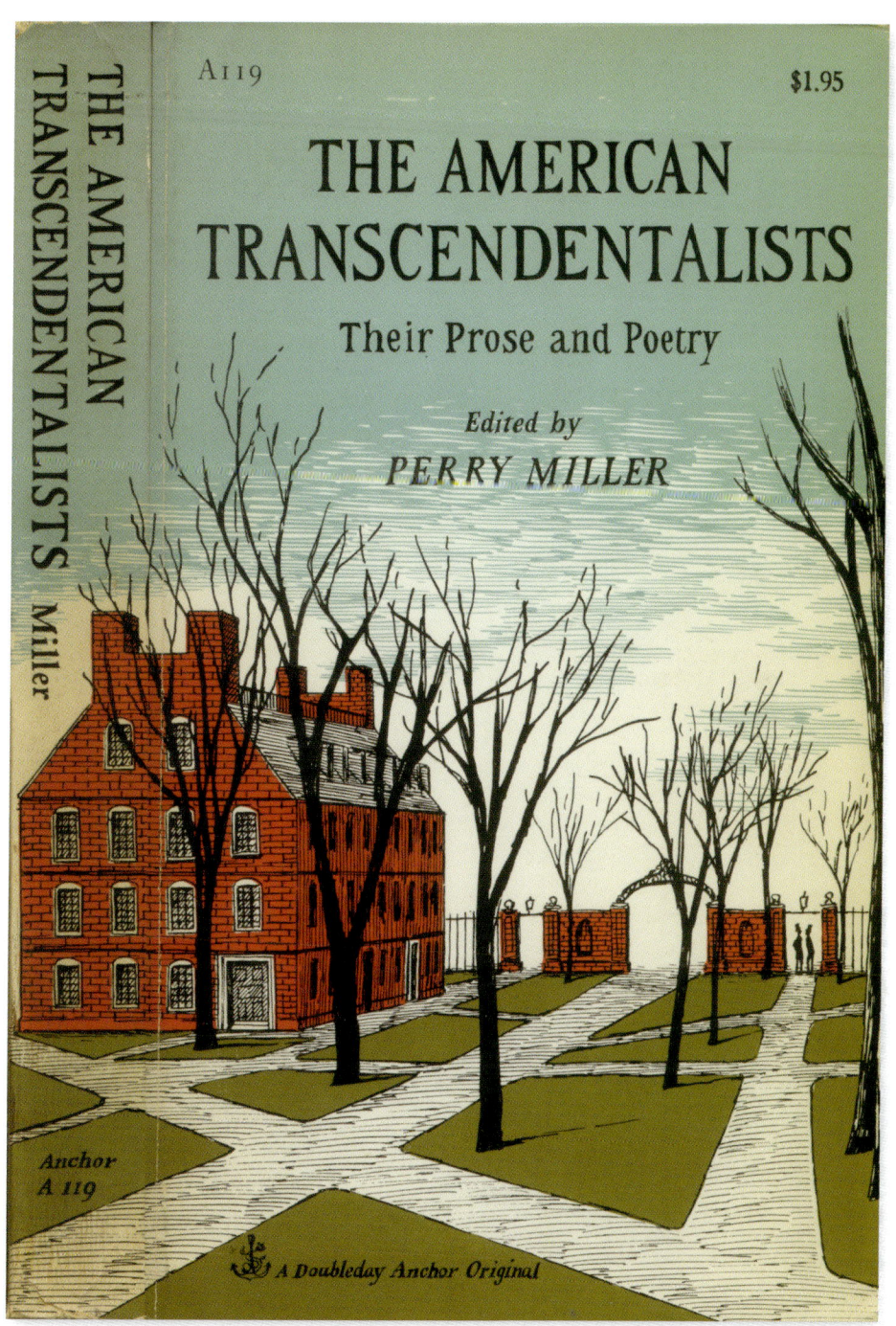

The American Transcendentalists: Their Prose and Poetry edited by Perry Miller
Doubleday Anchor, 1957, PB

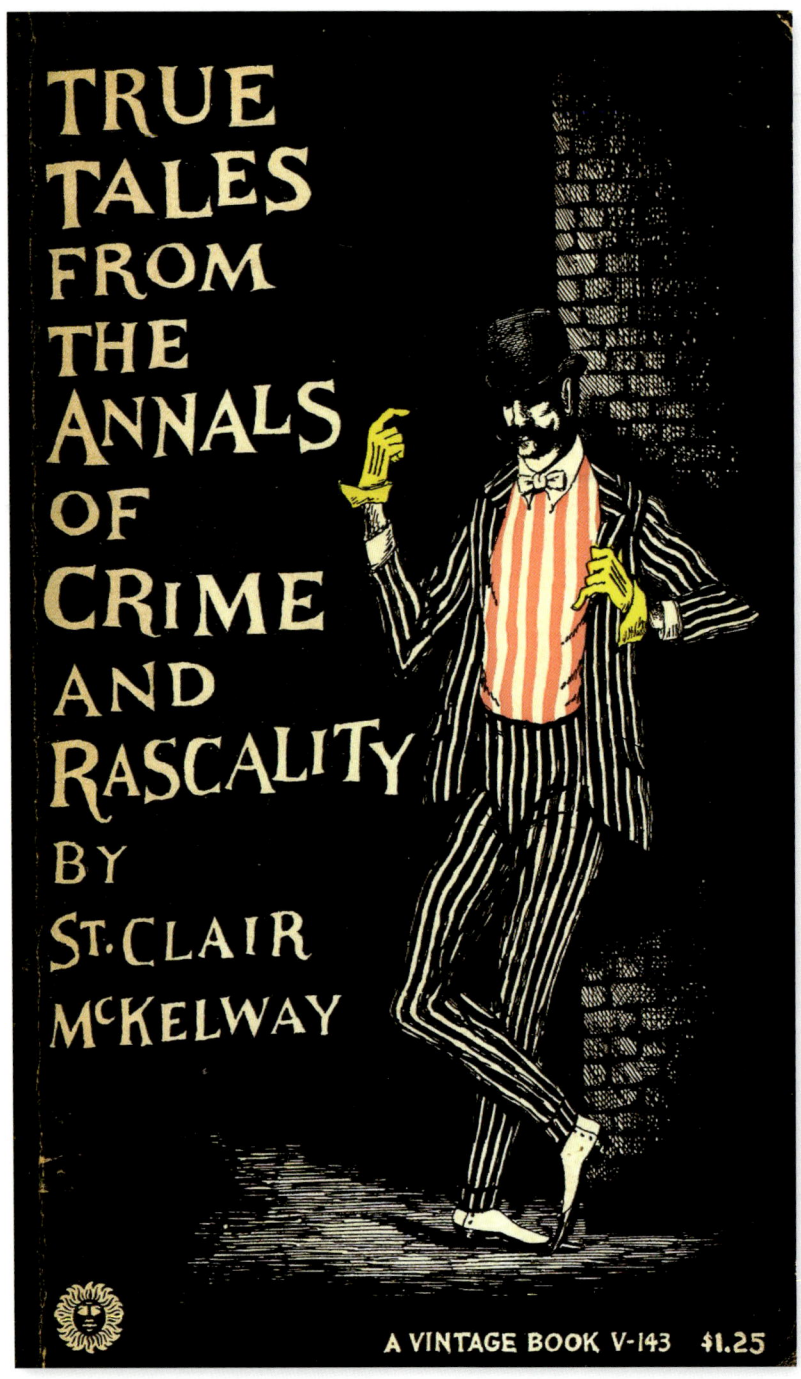

True Tales from the Annals of Crime and Rascality by St. Clair McKelway
Vintage Books, 1957, PB

Tales of Good and Evil by Nikolai V. Gogol
Doubleday Anchor, 1957, PB

The Awkward Age by Henry James
Doubleday Anchor, 1958, PB

The Autobiography of William Butler Yeats
Doubleday Anchor, 1958, PB

The Masters by C. P. Snow
Doubleday Anchor, 1959, PB

Nineteenth Century German Tales edited by Angel Flores
Doubleday Anchor, 1959, PB

The Black Girl in Search of God by George Bernard Shaw
Putnam Capricorn, 1959, PB

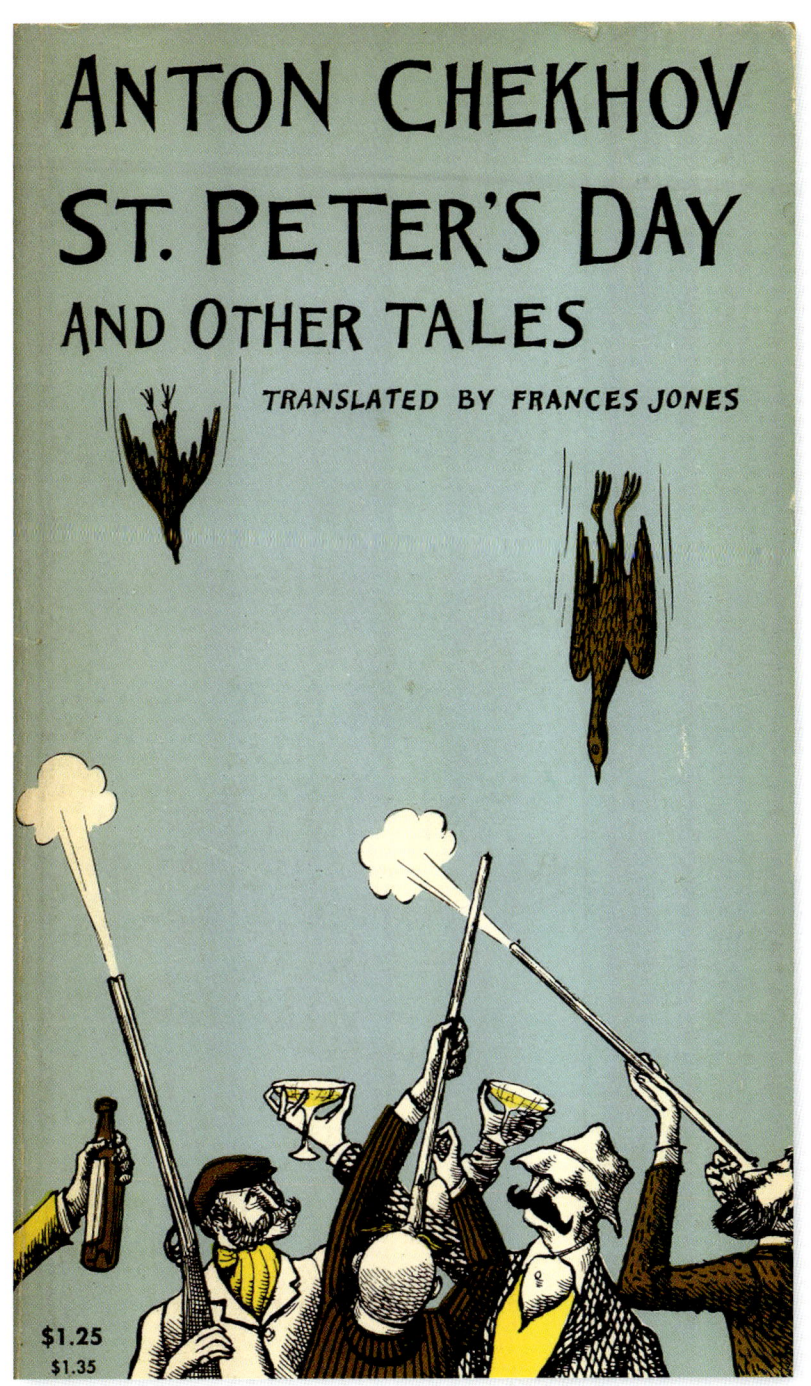

St. Peter's Day and Other Tales by Anton Chekhov
Putnam Capricorn, 1959, PB

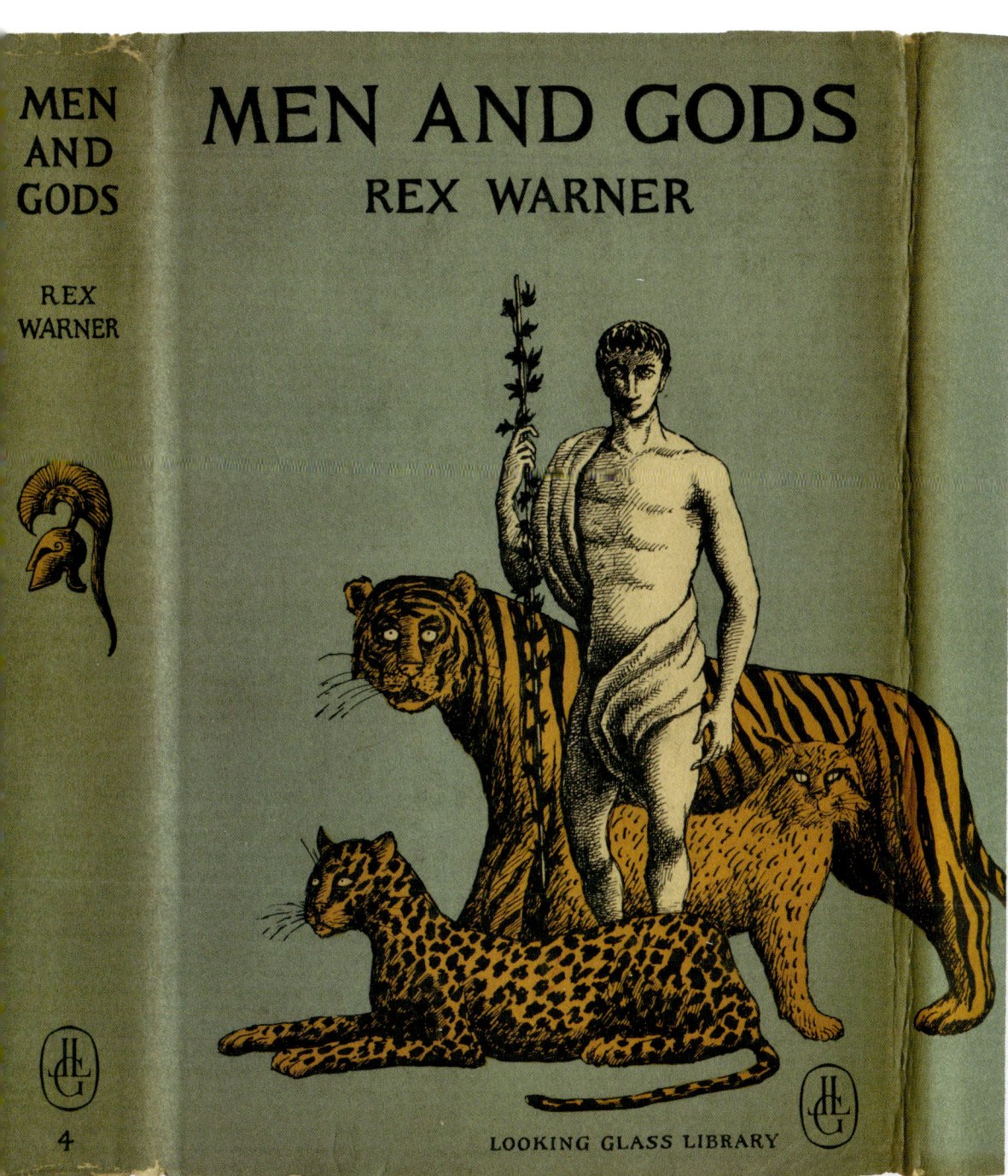

Men and Gods by Rex Warner
Looking Glass Library, 1959, HC, text illus.

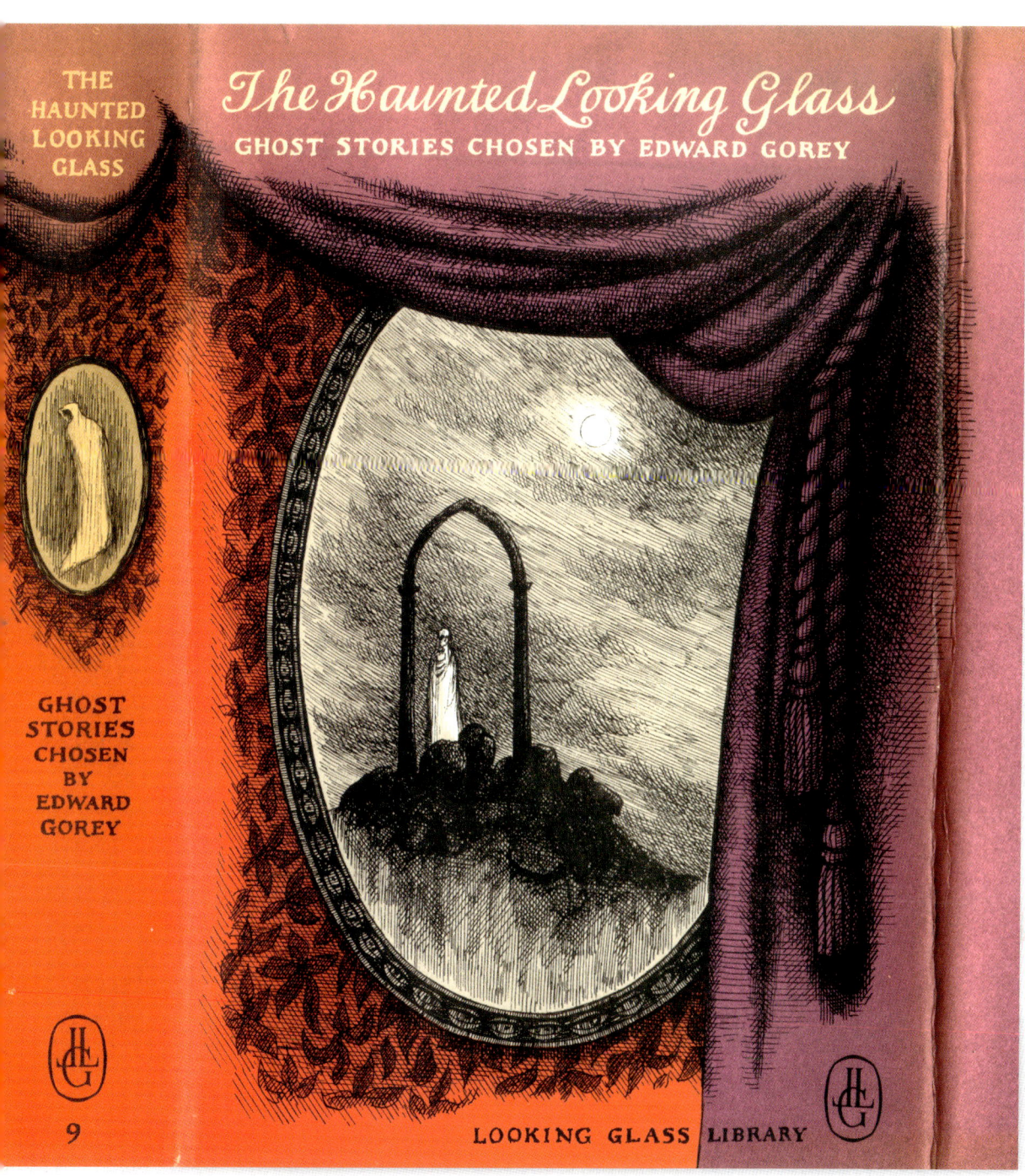

The Haunted Looking Glass: Ghost Stories Chosen by Edward Gorey
Looking Glass Library, 1959, HC, text illus.

The Man Who Sang the Sillies by John Ciardi
J. B. Lippincott, 1961, HC, text illus.

You Read to Me, I'll Read to You by John Ciardi
J. B. Lippincott, 1962, HC, text illus.

From Beowulf to Virginia Woolf by Robert Manson Myers
Charter Books, 1963, PB

Three Ladies beside the Sea by Rhoda Levine
Atheneum, 1963, HC, text illus.

The Innocent Curate by Paris Leary
Doubleday, 1963, HC

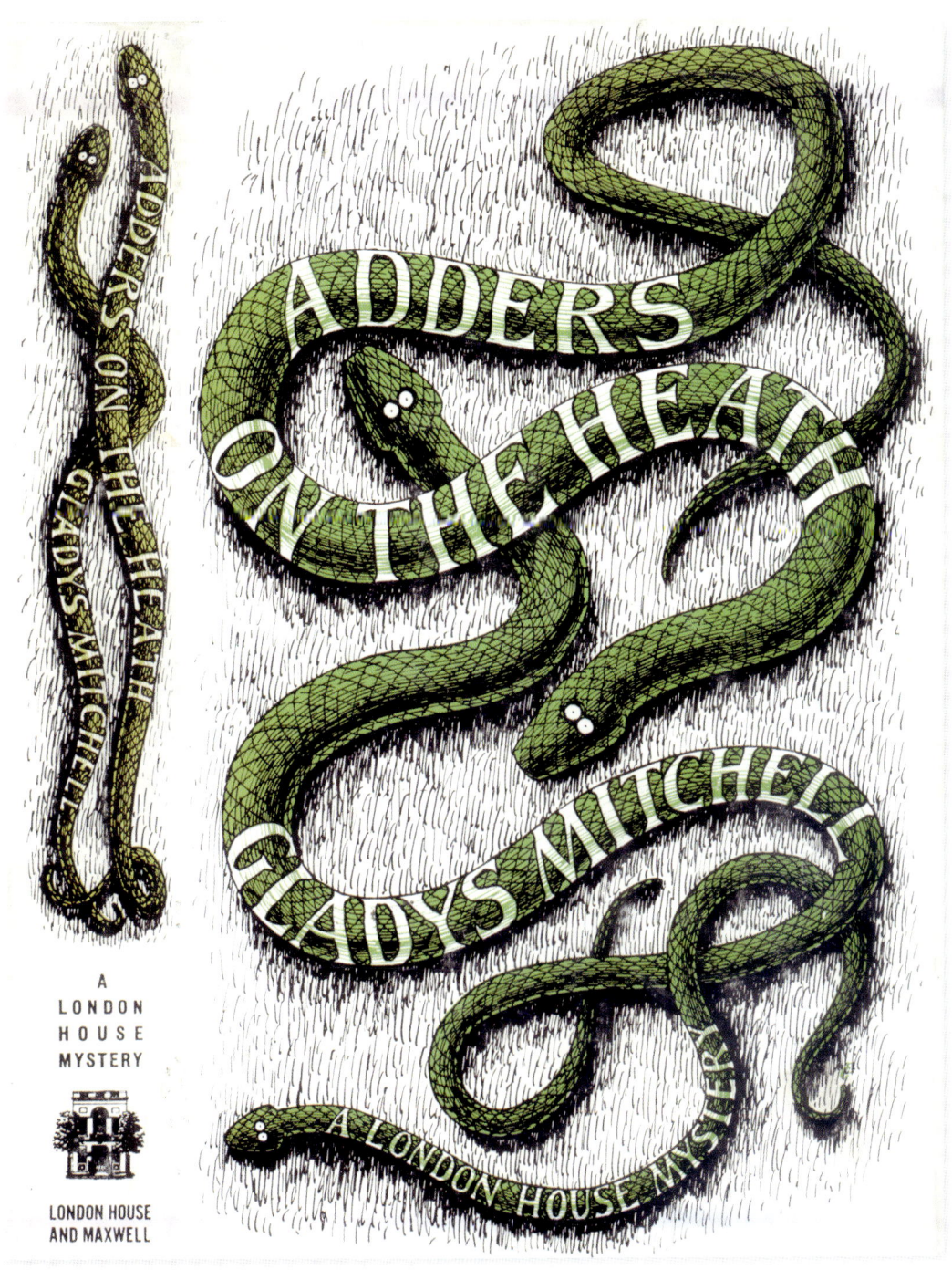

Adders on the Heath by Gladys Mitchell
London House and Maxwell, 1963, HC

Things: Stories of Terror and Shock by Six Science-Fiction Greats
edited by Ivan Howard
Belmont Books, 1964, PB

The Dark Beasts and Eight Other Stories from the Hounds of Tindalos by Frank Belknap Long
Belmont Books, 1964, PB

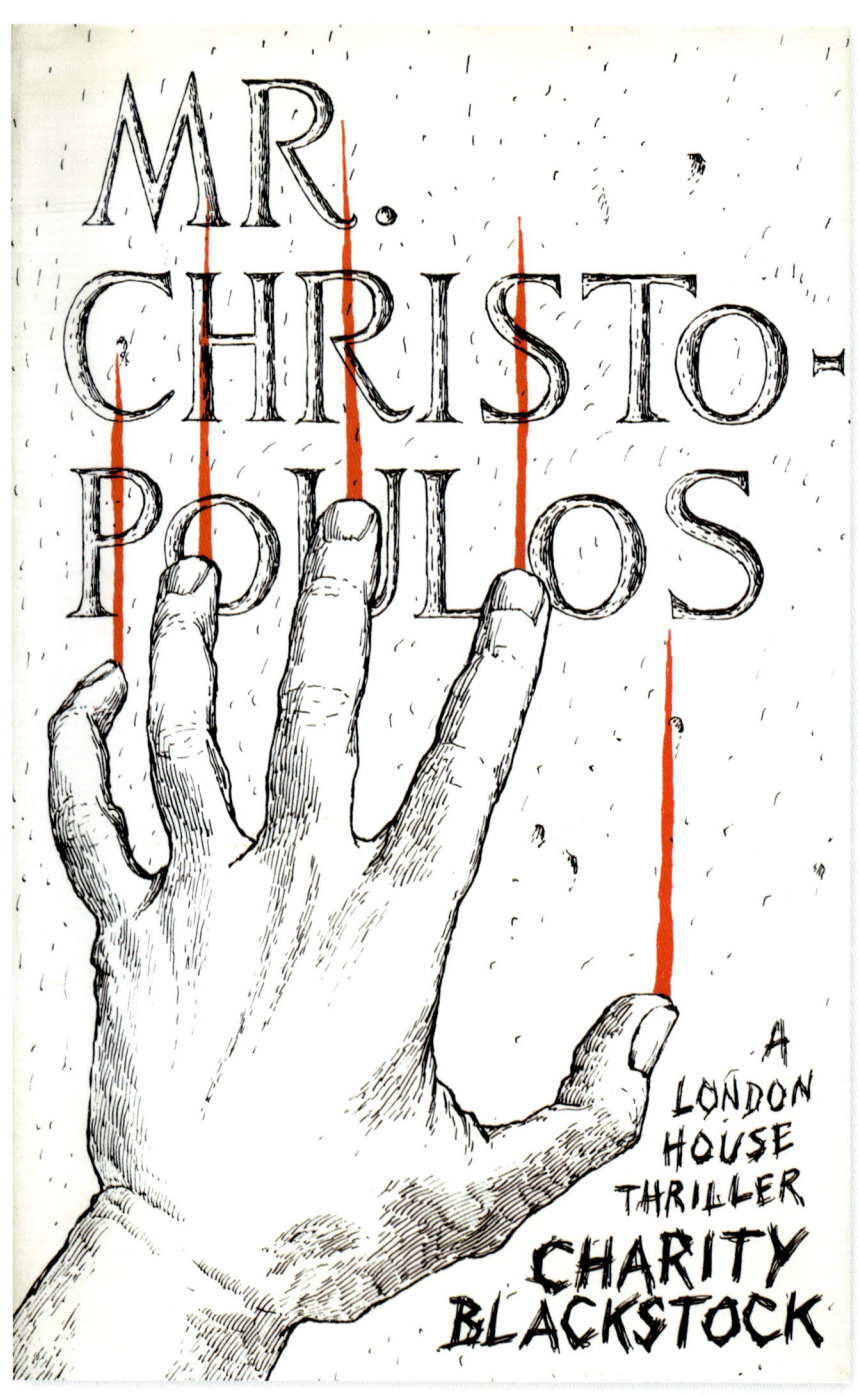

Mr. Christopoulos by Charity Blackstock
London House and Maxwell, 1964, HC

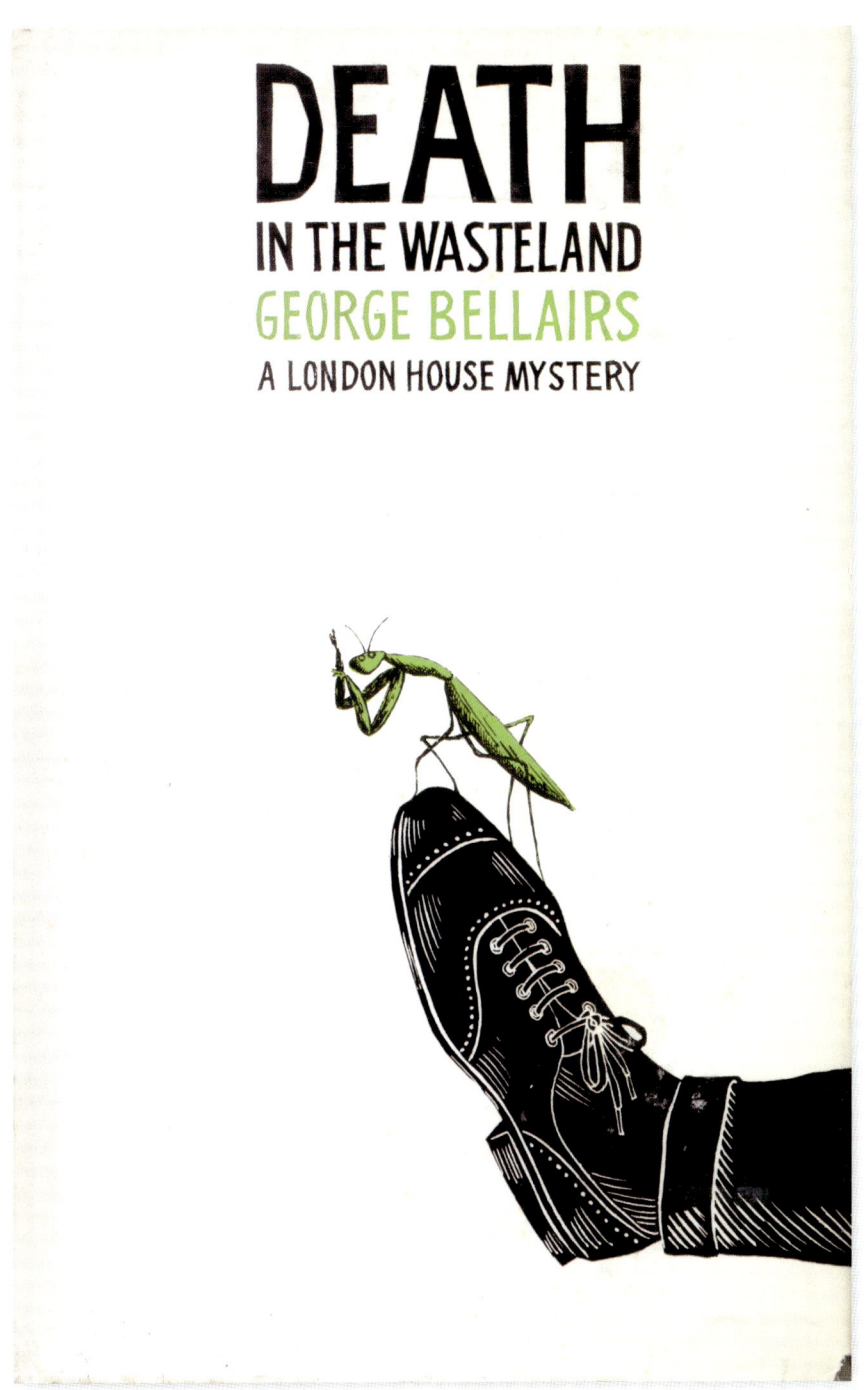

Death in the Wasteland by George Bellairs
London House and Maxwell, 1964, HC

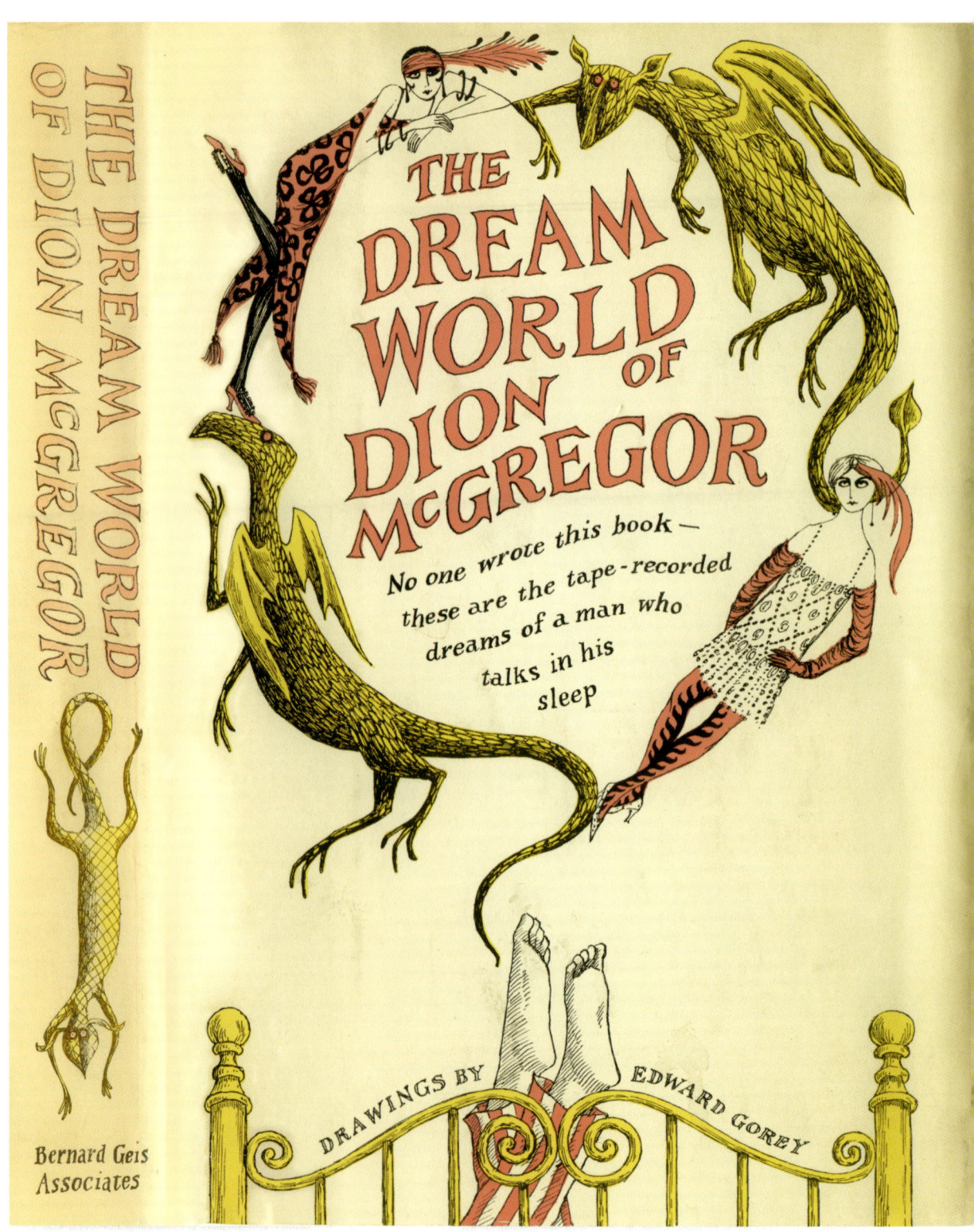

$3.95

A strange balloon voyage through fleets of sharp-billed storks—a wild ride on a trained flea—a classroom full of nude artists—

a perilous visit inside a giant's piano—a living Christmas tree—a mailbox crammed with un-openable letters—a walk from shore-to-shore across the water.

These are only a few of the more than seventy unearthly, bizarre, often hilarious tapes transcribed in this book. They are the dreams of a man plagued with constant sleep-talking and an insomniac roommate with a tape recorder. The result is sheer entertainment—and a fascinating glimpse into the private world of Dion McGregor.

The illustrations are etched in living dolour by Edward Gorey, author of *The Vinegar Works, The Muggly Wump* and other infamous books.

The Dream World of Dion McGregor by Dion McGregor
Bernard Geis Associates, 1964, HC, text illus.

Come Back, Dr. Caligari by Donald Barthelme
Doubleday Anchor, 1965, PB

Death of a Delft Blue by Gladys Mitchell
London House and Maxwell, 1965, HC

The Christmas Bower by Polly Redford
E. P. Dutton, 1967, HC, text illus.

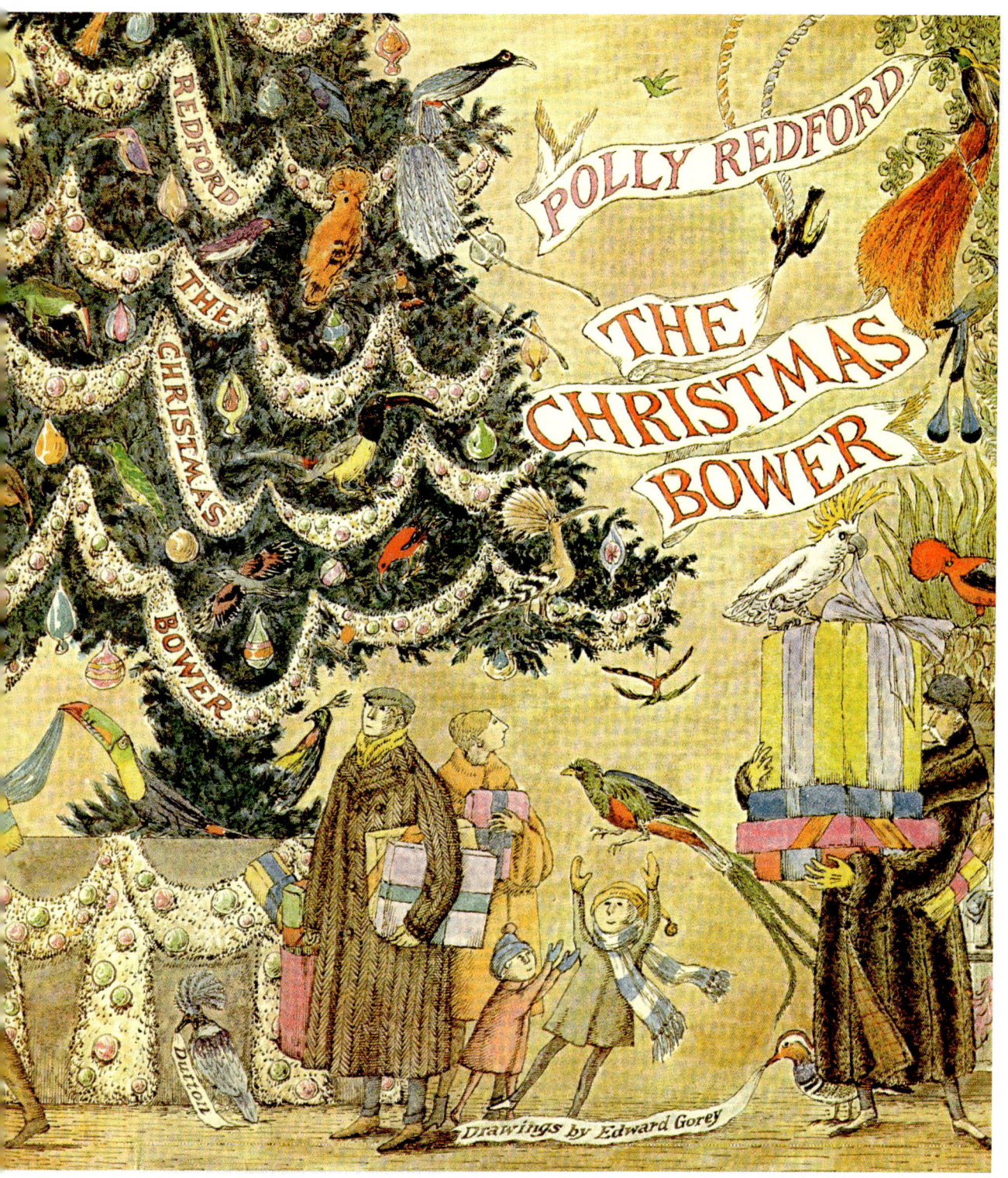

Cobweb Castle by Jan Wahl
Holt, Rinehart and Winston, 1968, HC, text illus.

Hauntings: Tales of the Supernatural edited by Henry Mazzeo
Doubleday, 1968, HC, text illus.

The Jumblies by Edward Lear
Young Scott Books, 1968, HC, text illus.

The Dong with a Luminous Nose by Edward Lear
Young Scott Books, 1969, HC, text illus.

Donald and the... by Peter F. Neumeyer
Addison-Wesley, 1969, HC, text illus.

Merry, Rose, and Christmas-Tree June by Doris Orgel
Alfred A. Knopf, 1969, HC, text illus.

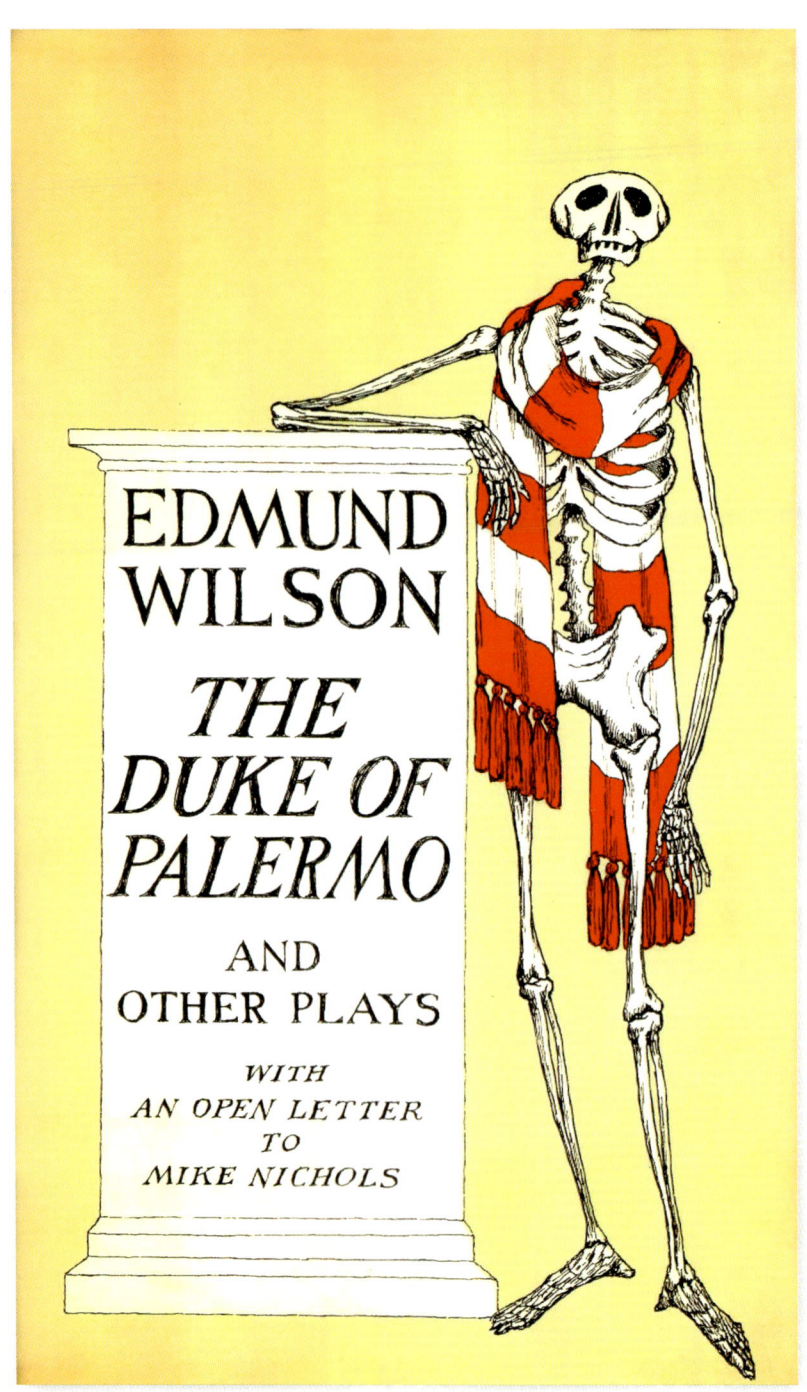

The Duke of Palermo and Other Plays by Edmund Wilson
Farrar, Straus and Giroux, 1969, HC

A Finger to Her Lips by Evelyn Berckman
Doubleday, 1971, HC

Someone Could Win a Polar Bear by John Ciardi
J. B. Lippincott, 1970, HC, text illus.

Miss Clafooty and the Demon by J. David Townsend
Lothrop, Lee & Shepard, 1971, HC, text illus.

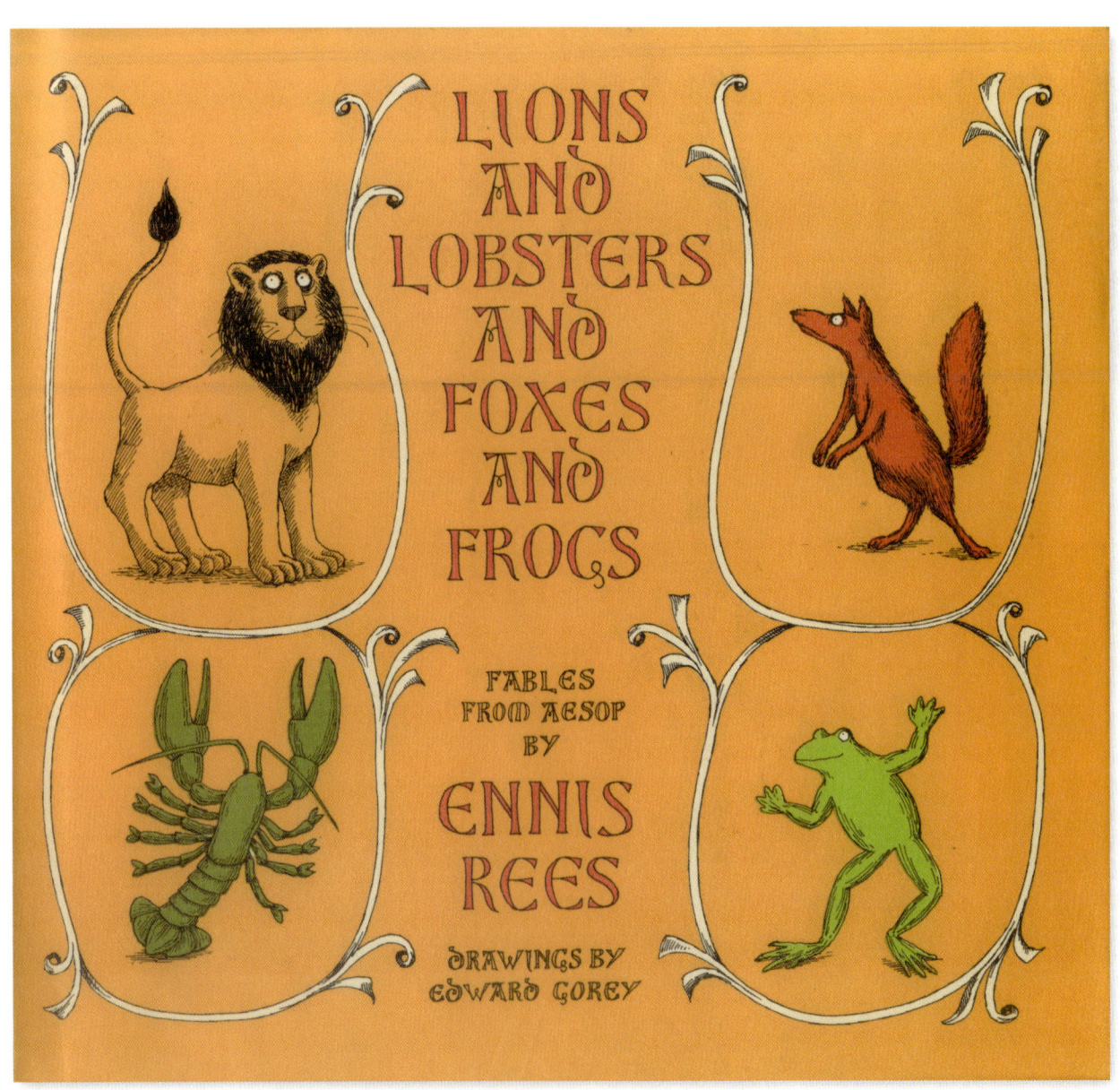

Lions and Lobsters and Foxes and Frogs: Fables from Aesop by Ennis Rees
Young Scott Books, 1971, HC, text illus.

Why we have day and night

Peter F. Neumeyer   Edward Gorey

Why We Have Day and Night by Peter F. Neumeyer
Young Scott Books, 1970, HC, text illus.

The Shrinking of Treehorn by Florence Parry Heide
Holiday House, 1971, HC, text illus.

Sam and Emma by Donald Nelsen
Parents' Magazine Press, 1971, HC, text illus.

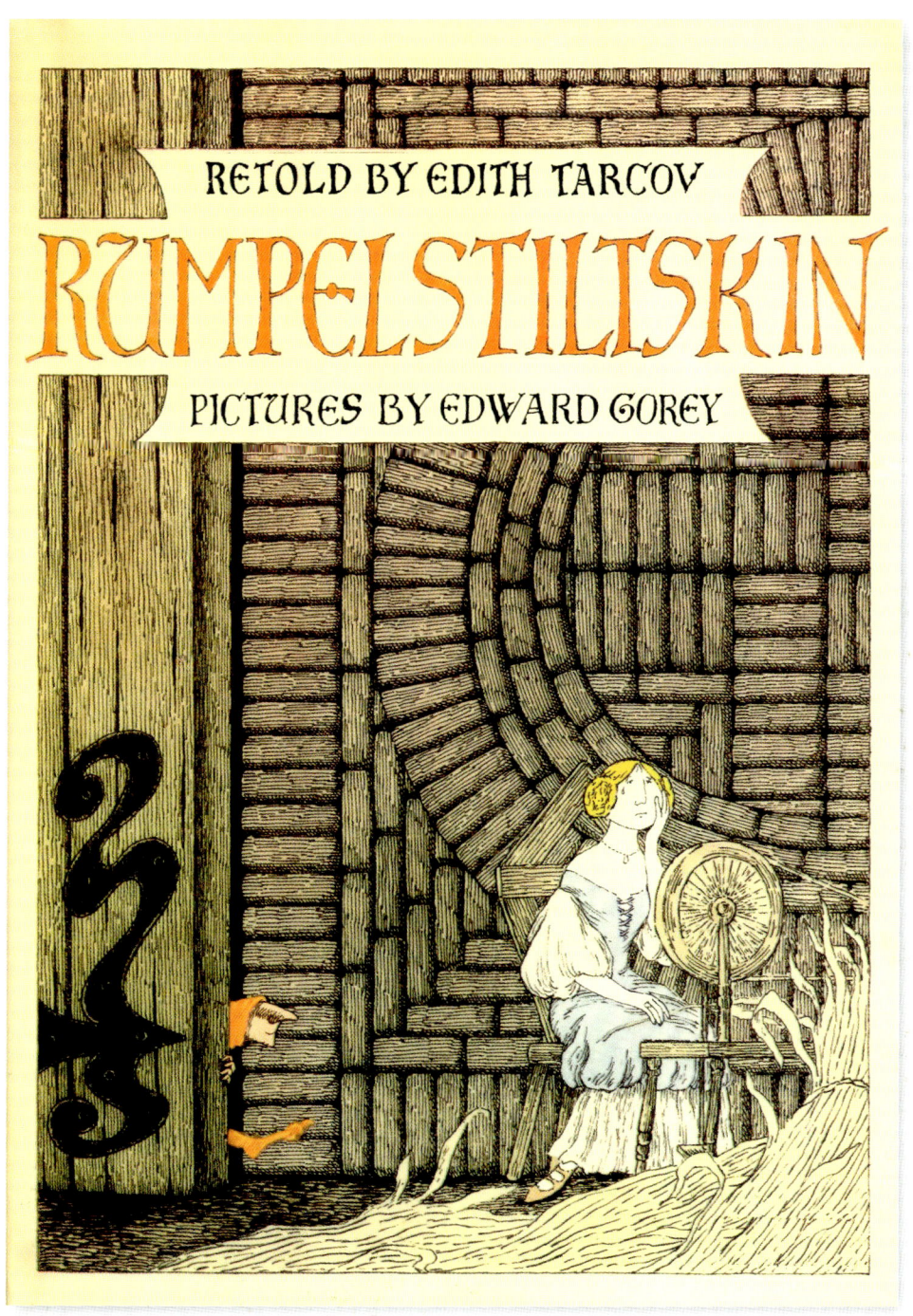

Rumpelstiltskin by Edith Tarcov
Scholastic Book Services, 1973, PB, text illus.

Grande Dames of Detection: Two Centuries of Sleuthing Stories by the Gentle Sex
selected by Seon Manley and Gogo Lewis
Lothrop, Lee & Shepard, 1973, HC

Limericks edited by Betty Jane Wagner (includes limerick by Edward Gorey)
Houghton Mifflin, 1973, PB, text illus.

A Song and a Diary for A by Richard Elliott
Adventures in Poetry, 1973, PB

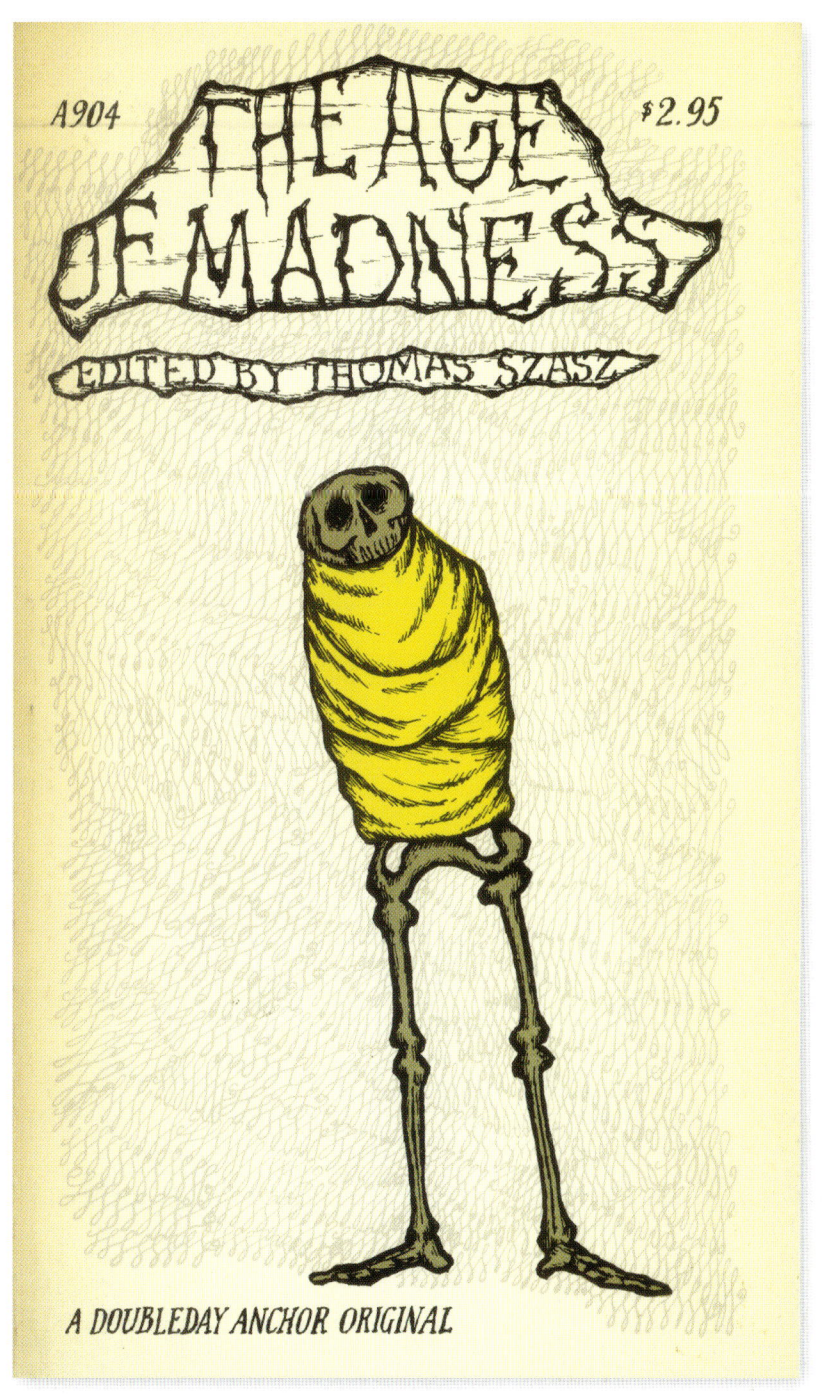

The Age of Madness edited by Thomas Szasz
Doubleday Anchor, 1973, PB

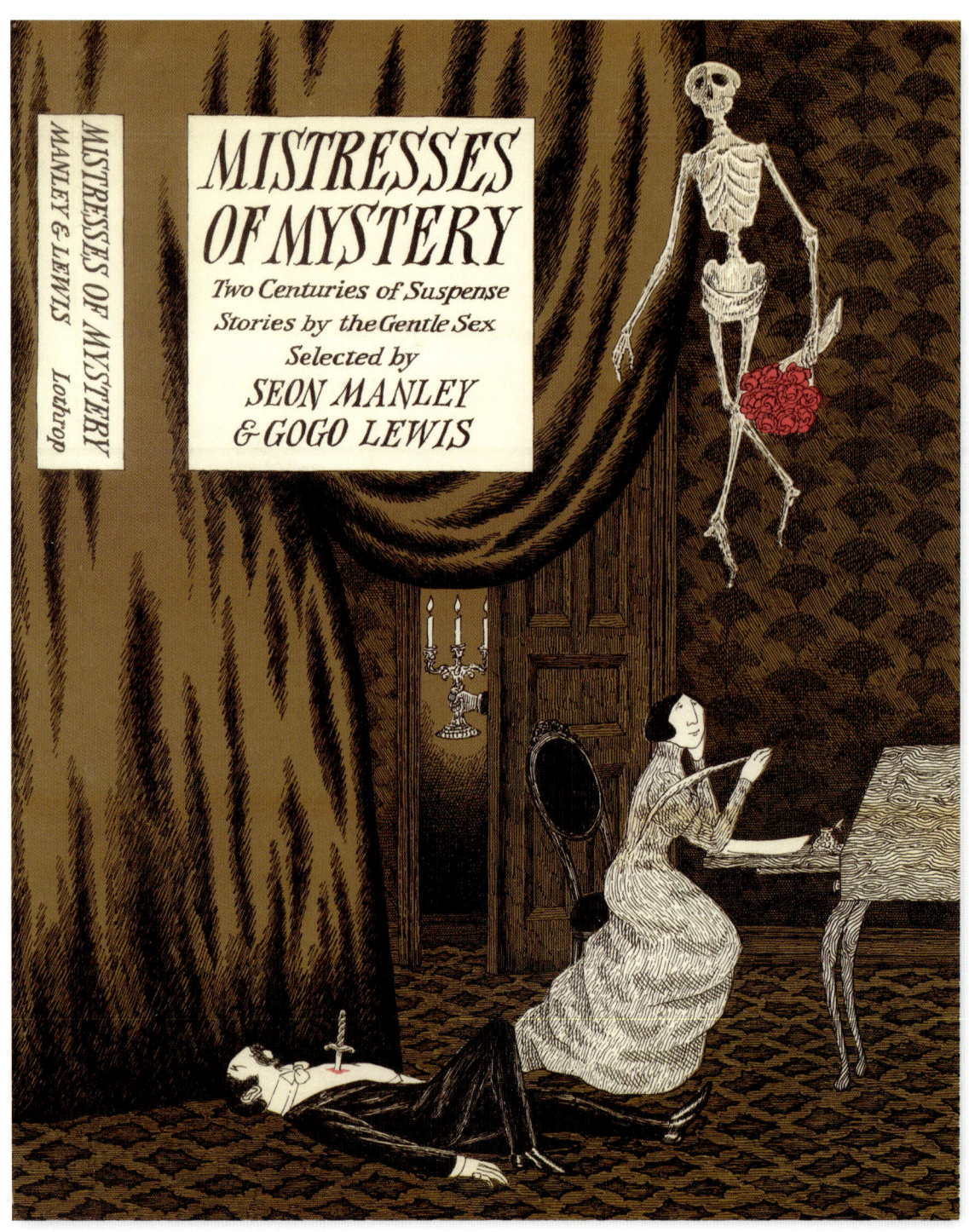

Mistresses of Mystery: Two Centuries of Suspense Stories by the Gentle Sex
selected by Seon Manley and Gogo Lewis
Lothrop, Lee & Shepard, 1973, HC

Limericks
Betty Jane Wagner
James Moffett, Senior Editor

The House with a Clock in Its Walls by John Bellairs
Dial Press, 1973, HC, text illus.

Other People's Mail: Letters of Men & Women of Letters edited by Lola Szladits
New York Public Library, 1973, HC

Phantasmagorey by Clifford Ross
Yale University Library, 1974, PB, text illus.

The Second Sin by Thomas Szasz
Doubleday Anchor, 1974, PB

Instant Lives by Howard Moss
Saturday Review Press, 1974, HC, text illus.

The Rats of Rutland Grange by Edmund Wilson
Gotham Book Mart, 1974, PB, text illus.

Edward Gorey's Dracula
Unpublished, 1979, text illus.

What Nigel Knew by Evan Field
Clarkson N. Potter, 1981, HC, text illus.

Devils & Demons: A Treasury of Fiendish Tales Old & New selected by Marvin Kaye
Doubleday, 1987, HC

Witches & Warlocks: Tales of Black Magic, Old & New
selected by Marvin Kaye
Guild America Books, 1989, HC

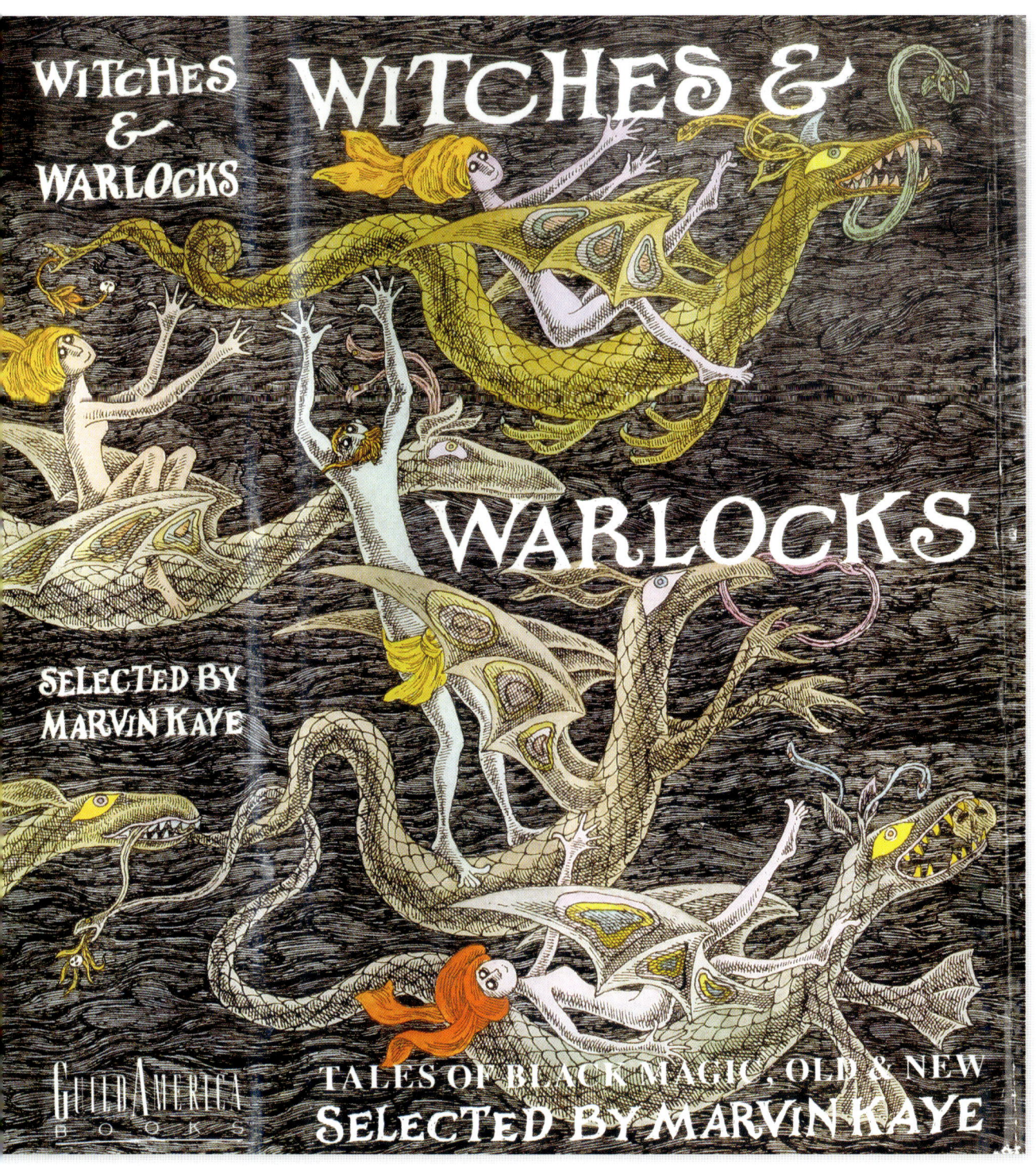

Haunted America: Star-Spangled Supernatural Stories selected by Marvin Kaye
Doubleday, 1990, HC

13 Plays of Ghosts & the Supernatural
selected by Marvin Kaye
Guild America Books, 1990, HC

13 PLAYS OF GHOSTS & THE SUPERNATURAL

SELECTED BY MARVIN KAYE
INTRODUCTION BY JOSÉ FERRER

The Twelve Terrors of Christmas by John Updike
Gotham Book Mart, 1993, HC, text illus.

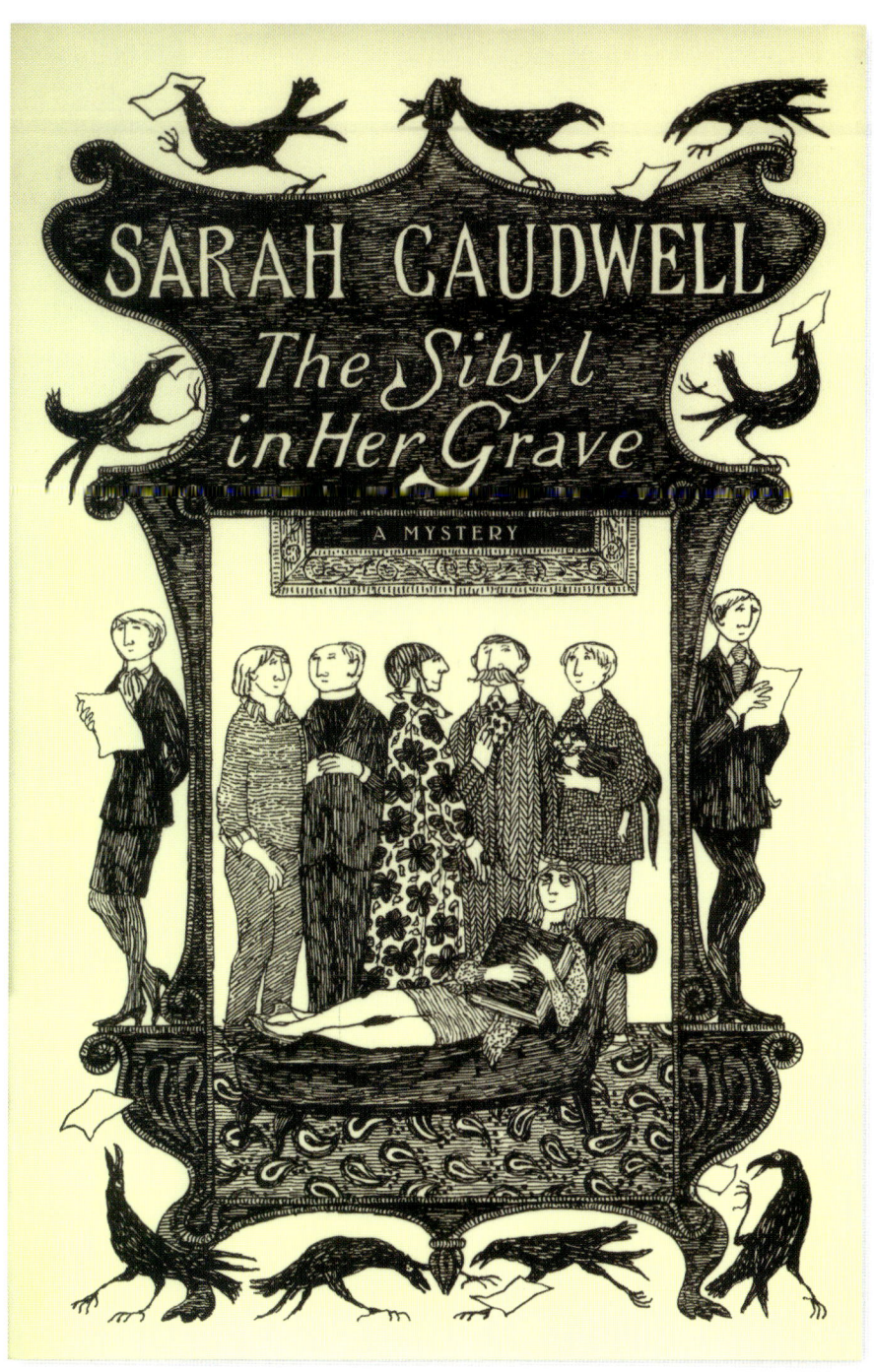

The Sibyl in Her Grave by Sarah Caudwell
Delacorte Press, 2000, HC

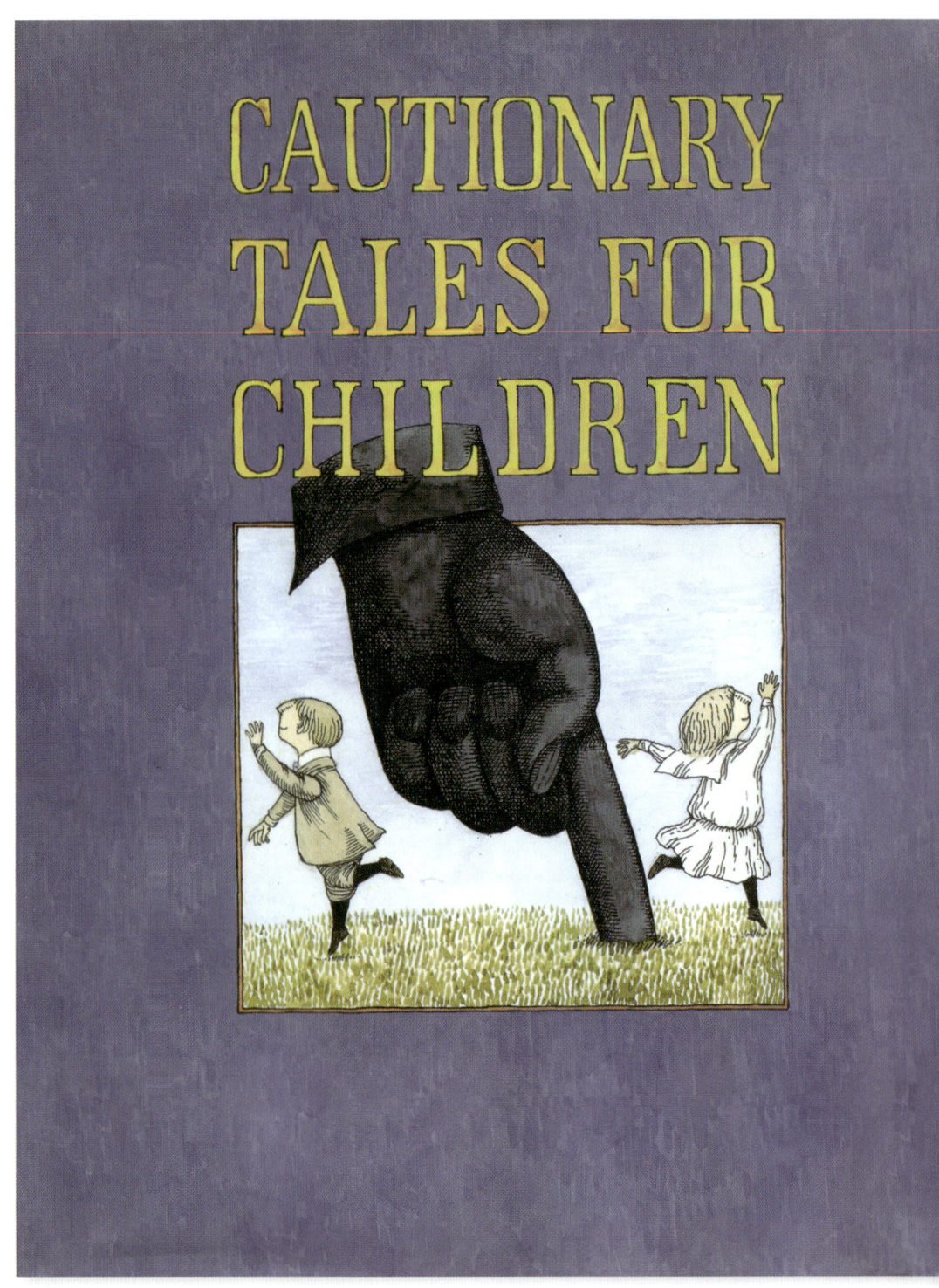

Cautionary Tales for Children by Hilaire Belloc
Harcourt, 2002 (illustrations c. 1989–1999), HC, text illus.

Index of Book Titles

Page numbers in italicized type indicate that artworks are discussed on those pages.

13 Plays of Ghosts & the Supernatural, 1990, 126–127
Adders on the Heath, 1963, 73
Age of Madness, The, 1973, 108
American Puritans, The: Their Prose and Poetry, 1956, 4, *5*, *21*
American Transcendentalists, The: Their Prose and Poetry, 1957, 51
Amerika, 1955, *14–17*, 18
Amphigorey series (not illus.), *25*
Ancient City, The: A Classic Study of the Religious and Civil Institutions of Ancient Greece and Rome, 1955, 39
Autobiography of William Butler Yeats, The, 1958, *17*, 55
Awkward Age, The, 1958, 54
Black Girl in Search of God, The, 1959, 58
Bleak House, 1953, 30
Cautionary Tales for Children, 2002, 130–131
Chance, 1957, 49
Christmas Bower, The, 1967, 82–83
Cobweb Castle, 1968, 84–85
Come Back, Dr. Caligari, 1965, 80
Comic Looking Glass, The, 1961, *23*, 24
Dark Beasts and Eight Other Stories from the Hounds of Tindalos, The, 1964, 74–75
Death in the Wasteland, 1964, 77
Death of a Delft Blue, 1965, 81
Devils & Demons: A Treasury of Fiendish Tales Old & New, 1987, 121
Donald and the . . . , 1969, 90–91
Dong with a Luminous Nose, The, 1969, *17*, 89
Doubtful Guest, The (not illus.), 1957, *23*
Dream World of Dion McGregor, The, 1964, 78–79
Duke of Palermo and Other Plays, The, 1969, 94
Edward Gorey's Dracula, 1979, 119
Either/Or (not illus.), 1959, *21*
Elizabethan Song Book, An: Lute Songs; Madrigals & Rounds, 1955, 42–43
Figbash Acrobate (not illus.), 1994, *25*
Finger to Her Lips, A, 1971, 95
From Beowulf to Virginia Woolf, 1963, 68–69
Garden to the Sea, The, 1954, *17*, 35

Grande Dames of Detection: Two Centuries of Sleuthing Stories by the Gentle Sex, 1973, 106
Greek Tragedy: A Literary Study, 1954, *11*, 12
Hamlet and Oedipus: A Classic Study in the Psychoanalysis of Literature, 1954, 38
Haunted America: Star-Spangled Supernatural Stories, 1990, 124–125
Haunted Looking Glass, The: Ghost Stories Chosen by Edward Gorey, 1959, 62–63
Hauntings: Tales of the Supernatural, 1968, 86–87
Hero of Our Time, A, 1956, *21*, 22
House with a Clock in Its Walls, The, 1973, 112–113
Innocent Curate, The, 1963, 72
Instant Lives, 1974, 117
It Isn't This Time of Year at All! An Unpremeditated Autobiography, 1954, 36
Jumblies, The, 1968, 88
Lafcadio's Adventures, 1953, *14*, 15
Limericks, 1973, 110–111
Lions and Lobsters and Foxes and Frogs: Fables from Aesop, 1971, 100
Listing Attic, The (not illus.), 1954, *23*
Loving, 1953, 31
Lucky Jim, 1954, 37
Man Who Sang the Sillies, The, 1961, 64–65
Masters, The, 1959, 56
Men and Gods, 1959, 60–61
Merry, Rose, and Christmas-Tree June, 1969, 92–93
Middle of the Journey, The, 1957, 47
Miss Clafooty and the Demon, 1971, 98–99
Mistresses of Mystery: Two Centuries of Suspense Stories by the Gentle Sex, 1973, 107
Mr. Christopoulos, 1964, 76
Nineteenth Century German Tales, 1959, 57
No Vacation for Maigret, 1953, 34
Object-Lesson, The (not illus.), 1958, *23*
Old Possum's Book of Practical Cats, 1982, *6*, 8–9, *21*

Other People's Mail: Letters of Men & Women of Letters, 1973, 114
Perfect Joy of St. Francis, The, 1955, 40
Phantasmagorey, 1974, 115
Pleasures and Days and Other Writings, 1957, *17*, 46
Rats of Rutland Grange, The, 1974, 118
Romance of Tristan and Iseult, The, 1953, 32
Rumpelstiltskin, 1973, 105
Sam and Emma, 1971, 104
Second Sin, The, 1974, 116
Secret Agent, The, 1953, 33
Shakespeare, 1953, *14*, 16
Shrinking of Treehorn, The, 1971, 102–103
Sibyl in Her Grave, The, 2000, 129
Someone Could Win a Polar Bear, 1970, 96–97
Song and a Diary for A, A, 1973, 109
Sot-Weed Factor, The, 1960, *11*, 13
St. Peter's Day and Other Tales, 1959, *17*, 59
Start from Somewhere Else: An Exposition of Wit and Humor Polite and Perilous, 1955, 41
Stendhal: On Love, 1957, 50
Tales of Good and Evil, 1957, 53
Thérése, 1956, *17*, 19
Things: Stories of Terror and Shock by Six Science-Fiction Greats, 1964, 74
Three Ladies beside the Sea, 1963, 70–71
True Tales from the Annals of Crime and Rascality, 1957, 52
Twelve Terrors of Christmas, The, 1993, 128
Unstrung Harp, The (not illus.), 1953, *11*, *21*
Victory, 1957, *21*, 48
Wanderer, The, 1953, *5*, 7, *21*
War of the Worlds, The, 1960, *23*, 26–27
Web and the Rock, The, c. 1950s, 44
What Maisie Knew, 1954, *17*, 20
What Nigel Knew, 1981, 120
Why We Have Day and Night, 1970, 101
Witches & Warlocks: Tales of Black Magic, Old & New, 1989, 122–123
You Can't Go Home Again, c. 1950s, 45
You Read to Me, I'll Read to You, 1962, 66–67